CW00370388

Encyclopedia of
Dog Care

BROCKHAMPTON PRESS
LONDON

This edition published 1997 by Brockhampton Press, a member of
the Hodder Headline Group PLC

ISBN 1 86019 708 6

Printed and bound in the UK

Contents

Introduction   9

Points to Consider before Having a Dog   10

Choosing the Right Dog   13

    Working, show or pet, pedigree or mongrel?   13

    Puppy or older dog?   15

    Dog or bitch?   15

    Choosing a puppy   16

Preparing for the Arrival of a Dog or Puppy   17

Keeping a Dog in an Outdoor Kennel   19

Settling in to a New Home   19

Dogs and Other Animals   20

Diet   21

    Manufactured dog foods or home-prepared meals?   23

    Feeding an adult dog—quantity and when to feed   25

    Feeding a puppy   26

    Feeding and rearing an orphan puppy   27

    Appetite loss in a healthy dog   28

    Feeding a dog during illness or convalescence   29

    Bones and chews   29

    Water   30

Training   30

    Learning to come when the name is called   31

    Learning to go to the bed or basket   31

    Sit, stay and lie down   31

    Walking on the lead, choke chains   32

    House training   33

    Training courses and specialist training   34

Routine Care of a Dog   35

    Walks and exercise   35

    Grooming   36

    Bathing   37

    Paws and claws   38

Cleaning teeth	39
Care of the ears	40
Eye care	40
Worming	41
Vaccination	41
Leaving your dog—boarding kennels	42
Insurance	44
Sexual Behaviour and Breeding	44
Male dog	44
Bitch	47
False or pseudo-pregnancy (phantom pregnancy or pseudo-cyesis)	50
Planned mating of a bitch	51
Pregnancy	51
Preparing for the birth of puppies	53
Behaviour of the bitch just before giving birth	54
Labour and Birth	54
When to intervene or call a vet	56
Routine care of the bitch and puppies	58
Behavioural Problems in Dogs	60
Aggression	60
Chasing cars and motorbikes	62
Destructiveness	63
Excessive barking	64
Eating inappropriate substances	64
Inappropriate sexual behaviour	64
Straying	65
Parasites	65
Internal parasites	65
External parasites	71
A-Z of Illnesses, Injuries and Veterinary Procedures	79
A-Z of First Aid for Dogs	139
A-Z of Breeds of Dogs	151

INTRODUCTION

The association of people and dog stretches back for thousands of years to the earliest human civilizations. Most experts accept that the enormous variety of types and breeds of dog that exist today are descended from a wolf-like ancestor (although there may be rare exceptions). There were (and still are) various species of wild dog sharing the environment with early human hunter-gatherer societies. In addition to the wolf, modern examples include African hunting dogs, Australian dingoes and North American coyotes. It is probable that early humans domesticated the dog in order to help them to hunt more effectively. Wild dogs are excellent and efficient hunters, as their very survival depends on this skill, and they increase their effectiveness by cooperating together in social groups. Hence the domestic dog is also a sociable animal, usually enjoying the company of other dogs or the human beings who take their place. Recent studies have shown that nearly all the behaviour exhibited by domestic dogs has its counterpart in the wild and, in evolutionary terms, exists because it helps the animals to survive and be successful. An appreciation of this is not only interesting in its own right but important for owners to understand. It is now realized that many behavioural problems (*see* page 60) in dogs result from the simple misunderstanding and inappropriate responses of people.

Of all the domesticated animals, it is arguable that it is dogs that arouse the strongest emotions in people. Throughout the centuries, they have been welcomed as faithful companions offering uncomplaining and unconditional affection, guarding the home and family, and sharing human labours and hardships. A bewildering array of characteristics have been selectively bred into the modern varieties of dog for the purposes of hunting, herding and shepherding, retrieving, pulling or carrying loads, guarding, guiding, detection or simply for aesthetic reasons. The fact that dogs can be used for so many purposes is a testament to their intelligence and versatility, and they have featured prominently in art, sculpture and literature.

Sadly, throughout history, dogs have been subjected to neglect, abuse and horrific cruelty at the hands of people. Today, mistakes are often made out of ignorance or a lack of understanding, and people, but especially dogs, continue to suffer as a result. It is the aim of all books such as this to help foster a happy and responsible relationship between people and their dogs.

POINTS TO CONSIDER BEFORE HAVING A DOG

It is worthwhile for anyone considering having a dog to take time to reflect on the decision before going ahead. Owning a dog is undoubtedly a responsibility but should be an enjoyable one. It is frequently said and accepted that the arrival of a first baby turns the household 'upside down' and life is never the same again. It would be an exaggeration to say that this statement can be similarly applied to having a dog, but animal rescue centres are full of dogs that have ended up there, no longer wanted because people have not been able to cope with the disruption in their lifestyle.

The first point to consider, therefore, is whether each member of the household really wants a dog, especially the adults. It is usually the case that the children in a family clamour to be allowed to have one, and parents may give in against their better judgement. While children generally retain their love for the dog itself, their enthusiasm for taking it out for walks in all weathers or feeding and grooming their pet rapidly wanes. Dogs inevitably generate some mess in the form of shed hair, dirt trailed into the house and the occasional 'accident', and this, of course, creates more work for the person who cleans the home, who is usually female! Articles left lying about may be chewed, especially while the dog is young. If the prospect of extra cleaning engenders a feeling of gloom and despondency, it is probably better not to have a dog. If the family has a baby or very young children, it is wise to consider whether this is the right time to introduce a dog. It can be quite difficult to maintain hygienic standards when a baby is crawling or at the stage of putting everything in its mouth, and the presence of a dog can be an additional worry. At some stage, the child is likely to sample the contents of the dog's bowl or have its face licked, and young children are most certainly at risk from some parasites that can be picked up from dog faeces. Obviously, with young children in the house, there is likely to be little time to devote to the needs of a dog. Also, a young puppy can easily be harmed or even suffer broken bones as a result of the rough play of a toddler or small child.

It is a good idea to analyse the lifestyle of the family and see how a dog would fit into the routine. Although many people have to do so, it is not really fair to leave a dog on its own all day while the family are out at work or school. In some communities, however, there are people willing to be 'dog walkers' or 'sitters' for a small fee, or there may be a neighbour who is able to let the dog out. The size and locality of the home should be considered, i.e. a flat or a house with a garden, in a town or country situation, and its suitability for a dog. If the decision is made to go ahead, then this will be of importance in choosing a suitable size and breed. In some new housing estates and in rented or council-owned property, there may be restrictions on keeping pets, and it is wise to check if any of these apply. A prospective owner should consider the feelings of their neighbours as it is not fair to allow a dog to be a nuisance to others. There is no doubt that a dog can be a cause for complaint, and it is not unusual for neighbours to 'fall out' or even end up in court over a family pet. It is necessary, therefore, to make sure that a dog always remains on your property by erecting adequate fencing or walls. Increasingly, regulations are being enforced to curtail noise pollution, and there are few things more irritating than a dog that barks incessantly, especially at night. Barking is less likely to be a problem in a dog that has been properly trained and given adequate attention, but the owner should be prepared to deal with it (and maintain good relations with one's neighbours) if it arises. (*See* BEHAVIOURAL PROBLEMS IN DOGS—Excessive barking, page 64).

It is extremely important to take into account the costs of keeping a dog, which can be quite considerable. As well as the initial purchase price and the few items that it needs, the major costs are food and veterinary bills. In general, larger dogs cost more to feed, but all require yearly vaccinations and regular worming, and there may be other veterinary bills if the animal becomes ill or has an accident. As with human medicine, an increasing range of advanced treatments are now available, but these tend to be expensive and, unfortunately, there is no National Health Service for dogs. Although there are a number of animal charities, such as the PDSA, which may be able to help in certain circumstances, it is the responsibility of the owner to pay for veterinary treatment. Insurance policies, which provide veterinary as well as 'third party' cover, are becoming increasingly popular but are a further expense for the prospective dog owner. If you do not have someone with whom you can leave a dog while you go on holiday, and are not proposing to take it with you, then kennel fees are another cost to consider. Once again, these tend to be higher for larger dogs and can add a significant amount to the overall cost of a holiday. It is also necessary to plan and book well in advance, as kennels are always busy, especially during recognized holiday periods.

All the above leads on to one final point, which is whether the people in the household are ready and willing to accept a dog and to make some necessary adjustments to their lifestyle. At least one person has to be prepared to exercise, feed, clean up after the dog, brush it, etc, and to get up promptly in the morning to let it out, sacrificing a long lie in bed. The fouling of pavements and paths with dog excrement is a great problem in towns and cities, and one that has become increasingly unacceptable. The person who walks the dog must therefore be prepared to clear up its faeces, although devices are now available that make this a less unpleasant task than it sounds. Unless very fortunate, the family will no longer be able to take off at a moment's notice for a day out or a weekend away without considering what to do with the dog. It is worth remembering that while friends and family may be delighted to see people, dogs are not always so welcome. Many public places open to visitors impose restrictions on dogs, and animals cannot be left unattended in a closed car for any length of time, particularly in hot weather. It can be seen, therefore, that the needs and welfare of a dog must always be considered by the family that owns one.

In spite of what may appear to be a long catalogue of reasons for not having a dog, large numbers of people are very happy with their pet, which can come to be regarded as a member of the family. A dog can be a lot of fun, especially for the children, and provides affection and companionship. It can be a great source of comfort for a lonely or elderly person, and the presence of a pet has been shown to boost the recovery of people who are ill. For those who have a dog, there is always a good reason for going out for a walk, which has positive benefits for human health and provides an excuse for leaving less pleasant tasks until later.

CHOOSING THE RIGHT DOG

There are several points to bear in mind before choosing a dog:

Working, show or pet, pedigree or mongrel?

A person requiring a working dog or who is interested in showing and breeding is likely to be well informed about the particular breed under consideration. Most of these dogs have a pedigree, and the success of their immediate forebears in working trials or in the show ring is likely to be of importance to the prospective owner.

The majority of people who want a dog, however, are looking for a family pet and often have a particular breed in mind. There is a wealth of information about each of the 200 or so breeds available in Britain, and, once again, these are dogs with a pedigree. It is a good idea for the first-time owner to study some literature about the chosen breed and, if possible, to consult someone who already has a dog of that type. All that then remains is to be quite sure that the breed is suitable for the particular home and family. It is important to consider such factors as temperament—boisterous or placid—usual reactions to children, size, exercise requirements and whether (as with the long-haired breeds) the dog requires a lot of brushing or clipping to keep its coat in good condition.

A note of caution—because of inbreeding over the years to produce what are considered the optimum characteristics, individuals of some breeds are more likely to suffer from certain physical or even psychological disorders. Inherited or genetic physical defects include a range of eye diseases, hip dysplasia, slipped discs and kneecaps, breathing problems, deafness, nerve disorders and a tendency to develop tumours (*see* A-Z of Illnesses, page 79). Responsible breeders of pedigree dogs do not wish to perpetuate these problems. It is important, therefore, to go to a reputable breeder, and the Kennel Club publishes lists for each particular breed. It is worth consulting a local veterinary practice, which may know of breeders within the area and can offer useful advice. Bear in mind also that it is often not possible to acquire a pedigree dog of a particular breed straight away. Much depends on the popularity of the breed, but a prospective owner may have to go on a waiting list for a puppy and travel a long distance to the breeder's premises.

Breeders should obviously welcome inquiries and visits from prospective purchasers. Many will wish to assess the suitability of a possible owner of one of their precious pedigree puppies, particularly as these may be in great demand. A pedigree dog is expensive to buy, although this may vary somewhat according to the breed. In any litter of puppies, there may be one that is considered to be less perfect, from the point of view of showing. A puppy like this may be less costly but will still make a perfectly good pet. A pedigree puppy will have its own set of papers, recording the details of its antecedents going back several generations. A 'Ch.' on the form indicates a champion in the show ring.

About half the total number of dogs in the United Kingdom are pedigree animals and the rest are crossbreeds or mongrels. Crossbreeds are the offspring of a mating between pedigree parents of different breeds, and mongrels are of mixed ancestry and may contain strains of many different breeds. These dogs can be lovely, affectionate pets and can be most attractive animals in their own right. Mongrels can usually be had for nothing as the owner of a bitch with puppies is often only too anxious to find good homes for them. While the excitement and prestige of the show ring are ruled out, most local dog shows have classes for mongrels and crossbreeds. These are great fun, especially for children who like to be able to show off their pet. Some people worry about having a mongrel puppy because they do not know how large it will grow. As a rough guide, look at the feet—large paws mean it is likely to be a big dog. By fourteen weeks most puppies are about half their adult weight, and at sixteen weeks most are two-thirds their full height. It is a good idea also to see the mother of the puppy, if at all possible, as this will give some indication of the eventual size. One commonly held belief is that mongrels are more hardy and less likely to succumb to illness. There is no real truth in this except that they are not so likely to be affected by the inherited disorders that afflict certain pedigree breeds.

Puppy or older dog?

In general, it is better to choose a puppy rather than an older animal, especially for first-time ownership. An older dog may be set in its ways and impossible to train, and usually takes longer to settle into its new home. It may have acquired bad habits that the new owners find unacceptable. It is only fair to say, however, that numerous honest, friendly dogs end up in animal rescue centres, unwanted through no fault of their own. Many people like the idea of giving such a dog a caring new home, and obviously it is best to take advice from those running the kennels. People involved in such work are normally highly dedicated and caring, and get to know the animals in their charge very well. They will certainly know if they have a suitable dog or will be prepared to tell you if one comes in. If you have children, it is wiser to telephone first and visit only if those in charge think that they have a suitable dog for you. Otherwise, the pressure on parents to take home an appealing waif or stray, whether suitable or not, can be considerable.

The people who run animal rescue centres want to find good homes for their dogs. If things do not work out, most will take the dog back, so taking on such an animal need not be daunting. It must be remembered, however, that some dogs end up in kennels because their previous owners have been unable to manage them. Others that have been neglected may be incubating diseases and are unlikely to have been vaccinated. Only people who are experienced in handling dogs and who know that they can cope without causing a nuisance to others, should take on a problem animal.

Dog or bitch?

Both dogs and bitches can be affectionate and faithful family pets, and more depends on the temperament of the individual animal and the characteristics of the breed than on its sex. On the whole, however, bitches make amenable family pets, being less inclined to wander or get into fights and more submissive and obedient. A bitch is likely to be a problem only when she comes into heat, which occurs about two times each year for a period of around three weeks. There are ways of coping with this effectively, all that is usually needed being a little extra vigilance in care and control (*See* SEXUAL BEHAVIOUR AND BREEDING, page 47).

In general, a male dog is more likely to wander from home, possibly for a day or two, especially if there is a bitch in season in the area. Owners of a male dog may find themselves being called to collect their pet from someone else's doorstep. A male dog may be less inclined to accept a subordinate position in the family, especially in relation to children. In the wild, dogs live in social groups, and each knows its position in the hierarchy or 'pecking order'. This is achieved by various behavioural displays—tail held high, pricked ears, raised hackles, curled lips, growling, circling stiffly —and sometimes attacks or fights. These may occur, for example, if a younger, hitherto subordinate animal becomes confident enough to challenge an older, more dominant one, but usually only a sign is needed to maintain order. A male dog may attempt to dominate children, but with correct training and discipline from the start this should not be a problem.

Choosing a puppy

Whether choosing a pedigree or a mongrel, the golden rule is to see puppies with their mother at the breeder's own home to be sure that the animals have been well cared for in clean surroundings, the character and attitude of the mother dog giving an indication of the likely nature of her puppies. If at all possible, the ideal time to visit is when the puppies are about five weeks old, when character traits are becoming established. However, no puppy should leave its mother until it is properly weaned, at about the age of eight weeks. The temptation to buy an appealing little puppy from a pet shop or 'puppy farm' should be resisted. These animals have already suffered the stress of being taken away from their mothers, often at too young an age, and have missed out on acquiring vital nourishment and immunity. If puppies have been brought together from different places, there is the risk of cross-infection with bacteria and viruses at a time when the animals may be stressed and least able to resist illness. A second move, even when it is to a good and caring home, is upsetting for a puppy, and it may be harbouring an illness. This is not intended as a criticism of the many well-run and caring pet shops that exist, which are trying to find good homes for the puppies in their charge, but merely to point out that there is an increased risk of problems arising in these circumstances.

When it comes to actually making a choice it is best to spend some time observing the litter as a whole. Ideally, the extremes should be avoided, either the most boisterous, dominant individual and the puppy that seems timid and frightened. Both may be more difficult to train and settle into a new home and pose potential problems. The chosen puppy should seem friendly, playful and interested in greeting visitors. It should not object strongly to being picked up and handled gently, or be unduly upset by this experience. It should be plump, with bright eyes and a healthy-looking coat and no obvious signs of any disorder. It should be neither thin nor pot-bellied, and the skin should be clear of any signs of irritation and should move easily. The experiences that a puppy has between the ages of four to twelve weeks are especially important for its social development. In the first few weeks, through contact with its mother and siblings, it learns to relate to other dogs.

Contact with friendly human beings, especially around the age of six to eight weeks, is important in establishing future good relationships with people. A puppy that has a bad experience at this age may show the effects of this in the form of some behavioural problem, well into adult life (*see* BEHAVIOURAL PROBLEMS IN DOGS, page 60). The best age for a puppy to leave its mother and settle into a life with its new owners is at about eight weeks. A puppy that does not leave its mother until later (three months or longer), especially if its contact with people is limited, is likely to have more problems in accepting a new home and family.

PREPARING FOR THE ARRIVAL OF A DOG OR PUPPY

As with a new baby, the items that a dog or puppy actually needs, as opposed to the things that people like to buy for it, are few and simple. Obviously, a supply of food is needed, and it is best to take advice on diet from the current owners. Offering the dog the food it has been used to will be one constant factor in the upheaval of moving to a new home and is likely to help it settle. Secondly, the dog requires a basket or bed in which to sleep that will provide a place of comfort and security. There is no need to buy an elaborate 'state of the art' dog's bed. These are designed to appeal to people as much as to provide a comfortable place for a pet to sleep and can often cost almost as much as the dog itself. An ordinary wooden box or drawer with no sharp edges, or even one made of strong cardboard, can make a perfectly good bed. A small, temporary bed is particularly suitable for a puppy because it is going to grow and probably chew its sleeping quarters. The bed can be discarded and replaced with a larger version as the puppy grows. For an adult dog, the main requirement is that there should be sufficient room to enable it to turn round easily and stretch out fully. It is easy to construct a three-sided wooden box bed with an open front, mounted on wooden runners to raise it off the floor. It should be easy to clean, wash and disinfect, and baskets can be a problem here as bits of dirt become trapped between the struts. The bed should be lined with layers of newspaper and an old blanket for warmth, which can be changed or washed frequently. Manufactured beds are often made from synthetic materials that are easy to keep clean or can be placed in the washing machine.

It is necessary to provide a collar for your dog with an attached tag carrying some means of identification, such as a telephone number. Other modern methods of identification include tattooing with an identity number or introducing a microchip beneath the skin on which details of ownership are recorded and also logged on a computer. These methods are particularly beneficial for valuable pedigree dogs to reduce the incidence of theft. They are painless to the animal but must be carried out by a veterinary surgeon. The collar must obviously be of an appropriate size for the dog, and even a young puppy should soon be introduced to wearing one. Along with the collar, a suitable lead should be bought, and there is a great variety of different types available. The expanding type of lead is particularly helpful at first, enabling the dog to run around without being let free.

The dog needs one bowl for its food and another for water, and it may be possible to find suitable ones in the home. The only advantage of manufactured dog bowls is that they tend to be of sturdier and heavier construction than those normally used in the home.

Depending on the nature of the dog's coat, it may be better to buy a special grooming brush and comb, but often an old hairbrush will do. Once the dog or puppy feels at home, it will probably enjoy having one or two toys of its own, and the children in a family will no doubt insist on it having them. Obviously, this is a matter of personal preference, but there is no point in overwhelming a young puppy with too many toys. It is a good idea, however, to provide it with something of its own to chew (*see* DIET, page 29).

KEEPING A DOG IN AN OUTDOOR KENNEL

The larger breeds and working dogs are frequently kept in outdoor kennels, but it is not fair to keep a young puppy alone in one for extended periods of time. The puppy should be gradually introduced to its kennel and given plenty of attention. Care should be taken in the construction and siting of a kennel. It should be made of warm materials, be wind-proof and watertight and be raised off the ground to eliminate draughts. Ideally, there should be an inner sleeping compartment large enough for the dog to stretch out fully and preferably containing a bench-type bed raised off the floor. It may be necessary to place the kennel in a shed to provide extra protection and to ensure that it is out of direct sunlight in summer. If the dog is to spend a considerable time in a kennel then it should be placed inside a concrete run enclosed by secure fencing. Newspaper and straw make good bedding for warmth and insulation but need to be renewed regularly. Both the kennel and run should be cleaned out and disinfected regularly and any droppings removed.

SETTLING IN TO A NEW HOME

Whether the new dog is an adult or a puppy, the main point to remember is that the animal is likely to be unsettled and anxious at first. Hence the approach is really a common-sense one of giving the dog plenty of attention and reassurance, combined with correcting it gently but firmly if it does something wrong. The dog should learn that its bed or basket is a safe place and should be taught to go to it from the start. Avoid overwhelming the dog with lots of activity, loud noises or numerous visitors before it has had a chance to get to know its 'family'. It may be necessary to curb the excitement and enthusiasm of children and to explain the dog's needs to them. The dog should be confined to its own home and garden at first and taken out on a lead. This is particularly important prior to vaccination (*see* page 41). Once it has settled in, has had a complete course of vaccination and has begun training (*see* page 30) so that it is sure to return if let off the lead, walks can be more adventurous.

A dog or puppy in a new home may be off its food at first. It is best to treat this calmly by offering food and then clearing it away after a short period if it is not touched, as a healthy dog will not starve itself. In the case of a puppy, it may be because it is missing its mother and former home. It may be necessary to tempt it to eat by offering different foods, as good nutrition is especially important at this stage. If the animal continues to refuse food, a veterinary surgeon should be consulted in case some disorder is present.

Dogs and Other Animals

Many dogs can be taught to accept the presence of other pets, particularly if trained from puppyhood to do so. A dog will often take a proprietorial interest in the pets of the household, even ones that in other circumstances it might be inclined to chase, e.g. a rabbit, as it regards them as belonging to the family. This is not always the case, however, and some individuals and breeds are more inclined to chase and kill than others. This is more likely to be a problem if one acquires an adult dog rather than a puppy, and a tendency to chase other animals should be firmly checked during training. Cats, with their tendency to wander at will, are the animals most likely to be chased by a dog. The habit should be firmly discouraged by giving a sharp smack if necessary. A cat that stands its ground, raises its fur and growls, or even takes a swipe with a claw-extended paw at the offending dog, can provide a salutary lesson although it is to be hoped neither animal is hurt.

Problems occasionally arise when a puppy or dog is introduced into a home in which an older dog is already resident. Usually the older dog is the dominant one, and the newcomer accepts an inferior position quite happily and without resentment, and the two get along very well. This state of affairs should be reinforced by always giving attention, food, etc, to the dominant dog first. Sometimes the younger animal may become confident enough to challenge the older one at some stage, which may result in some fighting and a change in dominance. Owners can help by not providing any support for the 'underdog' but always giving their attention to the dominant animal first, even though this may seem a hard thing to do. It is worth remembering that quarrels and aggression are more likely to be prolonged if the underdog is perceived to be favoured and protected, as the dominant one will feel the need to put the other in its place.

Dogs that live in the countryside must be prevented from chasing animals, particularly sheep. Marauding stray dogs inflict severe injuries or even kill many sheep and lambs in Britain, and a farmer has the right to shoot a suspect dog on sight. Training a dog not to chase sheep is therefore absolutely essential from everyone's point of view. Since sheep tend to run away readily and are easily upset by the presence of a dog, it is really best to avoid fields where they are present. Also, unless one can be sure that the dog will stay obediently close to the owner, it is safest not to let it off the lead in these circumstances.

DIET

Dogs belong to the order *Carnivora*, which means that they evolved to be flesh-eaters, showing adaptations of the jaws and teeth suitable for this purpose. They have large jaw muscles to give a powerful bite and well-developed, sharp canine teeth for holding and killing prey. The cheek or 'carnassial' teeth are adapted for slicing and shearing flesh. In the wild, all parts of the prey animal are consumed to provide the essential proteins, fats, vitamins and minerals needed by the dog for its daily life and survival. The stomach of a dog is adapted so that it can take in an occasional large quantity of food. Carnivores typically gorge themselves when they make a kill, and then rest and hunt again when they become hungry. It is now recognized that dogs, even in the wild, are also quite adaptable feeders and will eat plant material—berries, grains, fruits, etc—especially when prey is in short supply. Domestic pet dogs are therefore regarded today as omnivores and can be offered, and thrive on, a wide variety of foods, provided that their nutritional needs are met. Adult animals require food to provide energy for daily activity (including internal, metabolic processes) and for the repair and renewal of worn-out or damaged cells and tissues. Additionally, in young animals, food is needed for growth to build the structures of the body, which include bones, organs and tissues. The food requirements of a young animal are greater than those of an adult to allow for the demands of growth.

The protein in a dog's diet provides for growth and repair of cells, tissues and organs while the best, and most easily utilized source of energy, is fat. Carbohydrates also provide energy and, although not essential, generally form a part of the diet. Dogs require small amounts of vitamins and minerals, which are usually supplied in sufficient quantities in a varied diet. These are also present in the necessary balanced proportions in commercial dog foods and biscuits. A small amount of relatively indigestible plant fibre or cellulose provides roughage, which aids digestion and is of value in the dog's diet. Roughage, or fibre, is found in vegetables and bran. Some foods, e.g. white fish and chicken, are high in protein and low in fat while others, such as eggs, red meat and cheese, are good sources of both. Carbohydrates are found in a variety of foods, such as those derived from wheat or cereals, e.g. bread and rice, and also potatoes. As well as providing energy, fats are an essential source of fatty acids, which are necessary for many internal biochemical reactions vital for life. Of particular importance in the diet of a dog is linoleic acid, which is found in animal fats and vegetable oils such as corn oil. However, dogs are able to manufacture within their bodies the other two essential fatty acids, which are arachidonic and linolenic acid, and these occur naturally in animal tissues such as meat. In summary, 18–22 per cent of the dry weight of food should consist of protein, 5 per cent of fat and about 2–5 per cent of roughage, and the dog should have access to fresh drinking water at all times.

Manufactured dog foods or home-prepared meals?

Commercially manufactured dog foods are often prepared as complete balanced meals and so have the advantage of containing the correct proportions of protein, fats, carbohydrates, vitamins and minerals. They are designed to be highly palatable and are enjoyed by most dogs, and meals suitable for growing puppies are also available. They have a long shelf-life and, obviously, no preparation is involved. Guidance is given on the correct amount or weight of food to feed to particular breeds or types of dog. Manufactured foods are available in three forms:

1 tinned, with a high water content of around 75 per cent;
2 semi-moist in sealed, plastic bags, having a firmer consistency and a water content of about 25 per cent;
3 dried, usually available in strong bags containing small nodules of food and with a low water content of about 10 per cent.

Some types of manufactured food just contain meat and are designed to be added to an equal weight of a complementary 'mixer' food, usually of biscuit and cereal. It is always necessary, therefore, to read carefully the instructions on the can or packet. 'Special' diets are also available in manufactured form, e.g. 'light' mixtures for obese dogs that need to lose weight, mixtures containing higher proportions of fibre or fat, and those formulated for nursing bitches with special requirements.

Some owners prefer to prepare meals for their dog themselves, and this usually enables a more varied and interesting diet to be given. As long as a range of protein foods from animal sources is given, these will probably also supply sufficient quantities of fat. Suitable meats include beef, rabbit and chicken, and offal, particularly liver, heart and tripe, can also be given. It is usually better to cook raw meat, eggs, etc, as this destroys potentially harmful micro-organisms and their toxins and makes the food more palatable. Eggs and cheese are very good sources of protein, and fat and milk can be given in small quantities. A large quantity of milk often upsets a dog's digestion and causes diarrhoea. This is because adult animals are deficient in the enzyme lactase required to break down the lactose (sugar) that is present in milk. Dairy products are a good source of the calcium needed for strong bones and teeth.

Foods containing carbohydrates to provide energy, such as cereals and bread, can form a part of the diet and are useful sources of vitamins and minerals. Vegetables also provide vitamins, minerals and roughage but are not essential in the diet. Dogs are able to produce vitamin C within the body and so, unlike people, do not require vegetables and fruit. In fact, large quantities of vegetables are liable to produce digestive upsets such as wind and diarrhoea, but there is no harm in giving them in small amounts. Many dogs enjoy carrots, both cooked and raw, and can use the carotene these contain as a source of vitamin A. If feeding home-prepared foods, it is probably still best to include a daily amount of one of the types of available manufactured dog biscuits. These are relatively inexpensive and since they usually contain added vitamins and minerals, the dog's requirements are being met.

Since dogs are fairly omnivorous, it is possible for them to remain healthy on a vegetarian diet, usually one containing soya protein. Commercial vegetarian foods are available, but anyone proposing to feed a dog in this way should seek advice from a veterinary surgeon. A puppy weaned on to vegetarian foods would probably accept this as a matter of course, but a dog accustomed to meat might not do so well. In any event, great care needs to be taken to ensure that all the animal's dietary needs are being met and various supplements might be needed.

Whether fed on ready-made or home-prepared foods, a dog's meals can be made to go further with the addition of suitable scraps or leftovers. As long as the dog is being fed on a good quality diet, looks and appears healthy and energetic, and is neither gaining nor losing weight, it can reasonably be assumed that the feeding is about right. As previously mentioned, the dog should always have access to clean, fresh drinking water, which should be renewed frequently. Dogs tend to become thirsty after a meal and will drink more if fed a mainly dry diet. There is no need to offer any other kind of drink, although a small amount of milk is usually enjoyed by a dog.

From an early age, a dog should be given its meals in its own bowl, situated in a particular place, and should be discouraged from begging at the table when the family are eating. It can be difficult to insist on this when there are children around, but a dog that begs in this way can make a great nuisance of itself and it is easier never to start a bad habit than to try to correct one. If you want to give the occasional treat or reward, it should be away from the table and not at meal times. These items should not be of sufficient quantity to make any difference to the overall diet of the dog.

Feeding an adult dog—quantity and when to feed

The quantity of food to give a dog is something that causes anxiety for some owners. In Britain the problem is more likely to be one of overfeeding rather than underfeeding and, as with people, it is not good for a dog to be obese. The tins and packets of prepared dog food all carry guidelines on the amount to give, based on weight and using the different breeds as examples, which makes it relatively easy to judge how much to give. These recommendations can be used as a guide to those wishing to feed home-prepared foods. It is worth remembering, however, that guidelines are intended to be just that and are not a set of hard and fast rules. Individual dogs vary considerably in the amount of food they need, depending on how active they are. Dogs that are running about all day or working hard obviously need more food to meet their higher energy requirements and to their maintain condition and fitness. All dogs become less active in old age and require smaller amounts of food (about a 10–20 per cent reduction) to accommodate for this. It is particularly important not to allow an old dog to become overweight, as this is the age when the dog has an increased likelihood of developing heart, joint and other problems, which are made worse by obesity.

A bitch needs an increased amount of food (half as much again) during the last three weeks of pregnancy. While feeding a litter of puppies a bitch needs about three times as much food as normal and, because of the quantity involved, this needs to be given as several meals a day. Once again, the guidelines on the commercially prepared foods are valuable in these circumstances, and the mother dog may require additional vitamins and minerals, especially calcium, at this time. Veterinary surgeons are usually happy to offer advice on any aspect of feeding a dog and should be consulted if any problems arise.

It used to be recommended that an adult dog should be offered one meal a day, normally during the early evening. This is because in the wild, dogs, in common with many other carnivores, are 'gorge feeders', taking in as much as possible when they make a kill and then having a period where no more food is eaten. It is now accepted, however, that there is no need to stick rigidly to this, and some breeds and individuals may respond better to a different regime. The overall food ration can be divided to give two or more meals a day. There are circumstances where this becomes necessary, e.g. greyhounds that are racing, other dogs that are engaged in hard, demanding work, and nursing bitches. Offering small quantities of food more frequently can be valuable if a dog is inclined to vomit after feeding because it takes in too much too rapidly. Also, a dog that is on a reducing diet because it is overweight may feel less hungry if its food ration is divided up.

Since the advent of balanced dried meals for dogs, the practice of 'ad-lib' feeding has become increasingly popular. With this method, a quantity of such food is always available and the dog is free to eat when it wants to. Most dogs fed in this way take only what they need but some over-eat and become too fat. Dogs generally do not find dried food as palatable as the moist varieties. Some owners give one 'moist' meal combined with 'ad-lib' feeding on dried food.

In summary, as long as the dog is healthy and neither too fat nor too thin, it is possible to arrive at a method of feeding that suits the household and the individual animal.

Feeding a puppy

A puppy needs only its mother's milk during the first few weeks of life as this contains the perfect combination of nutrients. At about three weeks of age it is possible to start introducing other foods. A good one to try is baby cereal or bread mixed with a little proprietary formula puppy milk. Allowing the puppy to lick a little of the food off a finger, or placing a small amount on its tongue, may encourage the process. A meat or chicken broth with bread may also be tried as a weaning food. Once the puppy has become accustomed to the food, three meals each day can be given. Puppies may need to be fed one at a time to make sure that each receives a share of the food. At four weeks, a greater variety of food with a coarser texture, e.g. minced meat and fish, can be given, building up to four meals a day. By six weeks the puppy should be receiving most of its nutrition from four small meals a day, two of which are meat-based and the others of puppy milk and cereal. Commercially prepared puppy foods are very helpful to ensure that nutritional requirements are being met. The main point to remember is that new food should be introduced slowly and in small amounts to avoid upsetting the puppy's digestion.

The puppy does most of its growing between the ages of seven weeks and six months, and so needs plenty of nutritious food, and there is little danger of overfeeding at this stage. By twelve weeks, the number of meals each day can be reduced to three, one of which is based on milk and cereal and the other two on meat and biscuits. Obviously, as the puppy grows it requires proportionately more food at each meal. Between six months and nine months, two meals of meat and meal or biscuit are usually sufficient. At nine months to one year, the dog is a young adult and can be fed accordingly.

Feeding and rearing an orphan puppy

It is possible to rear successfully puppies orphaned at birth, but this undoubtedly involves a great deal of dedicated hard work on the part of the owner. It is advisable to try to telephone your veterinary surgery, local breeding kennels and welfare organizations to see if there are any potential foster mothers for the puppies. A bitch that has just had puppies of her own might be persuaded to accept another one, and this is the best option if it can be arranged. If this is not possible, the puppies should be kept in a box insulated with newspaper and lined with an old blanket or other suitable covering. The temperature should be kept at a constant 26.5°C (80°F)—a heat lamp can be useful for this. Also, a well-wrapped hot-water bottle should be placed in the box and kept constantly warm. The puppies need to be fed with a proprietary milk formula for the first three weeks of life by means of suitable bottle or pipette. At first they require small quantities every two or three hours, but the intervals can be increased after a few days. Each puppy should have its face and stomach gently wiped with a damp, clean cloth and then dried with a warm towel. This simulates the licking of a mother dog and aids digestion of the milk. Puppies reared in this way are very vulnerable to infection as they do not receive the vital immunity normally passed on in the colostrum and milk of the mother. Hence, as with a human baby, hygiene is very important and items used should be kept clean and sterilized. If there is evidence of an infection or digestive upset such as diarrhoea, veterinary advice should be immediately obtained. If only one puppy is affected it may have to be kept apart from the others for a time. Weaning can begin early, at the age of three weeks or even sooner, but the puppies will still require regular feeding with formula milk.

Appetite loss in a healthy dog

It is not uncommon for a perfectly healthy dog to lose its appetite occasionally and, provided that the animal is well in other respects, there is no need to worry. A healthy dog will not allow itself to starve. A dog may become bored with being given the same food day after day and you may wish to indulge it by trying something new. Gently heating moist foods to blood heat temperature increases their palatability. The best response is to not give any other food except the dog's usual meal. If the animal does not eat it, the food should be cleared away after about half an hour and a fresh meal given at the next feeding time. In this way, the dog soon learns to accept its meals at the regular time. Undoubtedly, there are some individuals that are fussy eaters but often this tends to be encouraged by anxiety on the part of the owner. There is no harm in trying an alternative, balanced and wholesome food instead of the usual meal. However, if you pander to the dog by giving it some more appetizing (and usually expensive) type of human food after it has refused its normal meal, then it is not surprising if it develops fussy habits.

Feeding a dog during illness or convalescence

Dogs, like people, tend to go off their food when unwell and loss of appetite is often the first symptom of illness. During the course of an illness or in the recovery period, it may be necessary to tempt a dog to eat something, and veterinary advice is helpful. A great deal depends on the nature of the illness. For instance, a dog that has lost its sense of smell and taste because of a respiratory disorder is more likely to eat a strongly flavoured food. Eggs, flaked fish, meat broth, baby and invalid foods are all suitable for ill dogs. Also, special, highly nutritious and palatable foods formulated for dogs that have been ill can be obtained from the veterinary practice. Serving the food at blood heat makes it more acceptable, and it is best to try to persuade the dog to take a small quantity at frequent intervals.

Bones and chews

A dog needs to use its teeth for chewing in order to prevent the build-up of tartar, which can cause dental decay and gum disease. In the wild, dogs chew and eat the bones of their kill, and this provides them with calcium and maintains the teeth in good order. Many pet dogs enjoy having a bone to chew but opinions vary as to whether it is a good idea to given them on a regular basis. Dogs do not need bones from a nutritional point of view and alternatives, in the form of chews, hard biscuits or crusts and toys, can ensure that teeth receive plenty of use. Bones can be positively dangerous in that they may splinter and cause damage to the gut, or fragments may become stuck in the throat, causing choking. The material may consolidate and form a dense mass in the bowel, which can cause constipation. If a bone is given, it should be part of a large limb or marrow bone. It should be given raw, as cooking renders bones more liable to fragment, and taken away as soon as it shows any signs of splintering.

In summary, although chewing and eating bones is natural for dogs, it is not necessarily desirable and can cause damage or even death. Plenty of alternatives and substitutes are readily available and should be provided to maintain the teeth in good order. This is particularly important for dogs that mainly eat soft, wet foods.

Water

As already stated, a dog should have unlimited access to fresh drinking water and will be especially thirsty a short time after eating its food and in hot weather. A dog can soon become dehydrated if it is not allowed to replenish water that has been lost from the body. The only exception to this is if the dog has been vomiting (*see* page 138), which is usually the result of an irritation of the stomach lining. The animal feels thirsty, but allowing it to drink a large quantity of water immediately may cause it to vomit again. This, in fact, causes a greater loss of fluid and minerals and a higher risk of dehydration. It is best to wait a while (about two hours) and then offer a small quantity of water. If this stays down, further small amounts can be given every hour. It should be emphasized that this applies only to mild cases. Severe vomiting is a sign of illness that requires immediate veterinary treatment.

TRAINING

Ideally, training should begin as soon as you acquire a puppy, at about eight weeks of age. An older puppy more than six months of age or an adult dog has already acquired habits and behaviour patterns that may be hard to correct. This is one of the drawbacks of taking on an older dog but, even so, with time and patience individuals may respond well and will generally wish to please. The main point to remember is to be consistent in correcting behaviour each time it appears, otherwise the dog will just be confused. For example, push the animal down gently and say 'No' each time it jumps up, and do not allow it to do this one moment and not the next. The other essential factor is to realize that dogs do not have a good memory. It is necessary to correct bad behaviour at the moment it occurs and when you see it happening rather than later on. The dog will know it has displeased you if you speak sternly to it while showing it the evidence of its misdemeanour, but it is doubtful whether it understands what it has done wrong. The most successful approach is to reward good behaviour and obedience with praise, correct undesirable habits consistently when you witness them but ignore, as far as possible, minor mistakes.

There are a few basic goals of training that it is desirable to achieve as soon as possible.

1. Learning to come when the name is called

As soon as the dog arrives in its new home, it should get used to coming in response to its name being called. Choose a simple, clear name that it can learn more easily. Reward the dog with affection and praise each time it comes when called. An older dog may be more independent and less inclined to respond. It is best to persevere and possibly reward the dog with a small titbit when it does return at first, as well as lots of praise. However exasperated you may feel, you should never smack or punish the dog when it returns after a long absence. This has the opposite effect of making it less likely to return the next time. It may be worth trying an extendible, running lead and calling the dog when it reaches the full extent of the line, accompanied by a sharp tug on the collar. A dog that takes its time about returning, or disappears to do its own thing, is a great nuisance to its owner. It is not acceptable simply to return home and leave the dog to come back in its own time, as it may cause problems for other people or animals. If a dog really cannot be trusted to come back, it is best to take it for walks on an extending lead (so it can still run about to a certain extent) and give it freedom only in the security of the home garden.

2. Learning to go to the bed or basket

From the beginning, the puppy or dog should feel that its bed is a place of warmth, comfort and security. Use a simple command such as 'Go to your bed' and place the dog in it if necessary. The command 'Stay' can then be used to teach the dog to remain there. A word of praise is appropriate, but if this is too lavish the dog may feel encouraged to leave its bed and come to you.

3. Sit, stay and lie down

A dog can be taught to sit by pressing down firmly but gently on its hindquarters, accompanied by the word of command. Once the dog has learnt this, it can be taught to 'stay' by giving this instruction while the dog is in a sitting position and walking a short distance away. If the dog follows, it should be returned to the spot from which it has moved and the process repeated. The distance may be gradually increased and the dog can be called and praised as it learns to obey. It is a good idea for the dog to sit and stay while its meal is put out and remain until it is called to come and eat. A dog can be taught to associate 'lie down' with the appropriate action, if you repeat this when it occurs naturally. You should not press down on the dog's back or shoulders or try to force the action physically as this might cause harm. If a stern voice is used, the dog will normally crouch down and adopt a submissive posture so this will be mastered with time and perseverance.

4. Walking on the lead, choke chains

A well-trained dog should walk 'to heel' (i.e. level with its owner's leg) on the left-hand side of the person's body. It should also sit whenever its owner comes to a halt, especially at a kerb before crossing a road. It is best to start teaching a puppy to walk on the lead right from the start, although proper training usually commences at the age of about four months. To begin training, the dog should be told to sit at the owner's left-hand side. The lead is held in the right hand, passing across the front of the person's body. The owner should then begin to walk forward, giving the dog an instruction to 'heel'. If, as usually happens at first, the dog rushes forwards and pulls, the owner should give a sharp tug backwards, using the left hand down the length of the lead and repeating the command. This procedure should be carried out each time the dog attempts to pull. A rolled-up newspaper can be used to give the dog a *gentle* tap on its nose while it is being pulled back, to reinforce the lesson.

With an older dog, it may be necessary to use a 'choke chain', which tightens on the animal's neck when pulled. It must be emphasized, however, that these can cause damage and injury, especially to a small or young dog, if not used correctly. If a choke chain is used, it must be of a size appropriate to the dog and constructed with wide links. It is essential that it is put on the neck correctly (*see* illustrations) as otherwise it will not release after it is pulled. The length of chain has a larger ring at either end. A loop of chain is fed through one ring and pulled until the two rings meet. One ring now appears to be on the outside and stopping the progress of the other, and it is to this that the clip of the lead is attached.

A choke chain is a valuable aid in the training of a large or unruly dog and is perfectly acceptable if used correctly. Since the sensation of the chain tightening is an unpleasant one, the dog is more likely to learn quickly to come to heel without pulling.

Correct fitting of a choke chain

Incorrect fitting of a choke chain

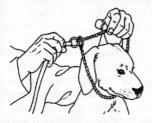
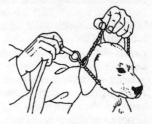

The loop of chain should be placed so that it runs from the outer ring with attached lead through the second ring on the right side of the dog's head behind the ear. It passes across the back of the neck to the left ear and then beneath the throat, ascending on the right side again to the free-running ring.

If wrongly positioned, the chain will appear to be descending from the lead ring through the free-running ring on the right-hand side and on beneath the throat. In this position, the chain is dangerous as it will not release when pulled.

House training

In the early weeks of a puppy's life, all its bodily excretions are cleaned up by the licking of the mother dog. At around three weeks of age the puppy has begun to leave its bed in order to relieve itself at a place close by. By the time it is eight weeks old the puppy will start to use particular places away from its feeding bowl and bed. By now it is beginning to indicate what it is about to do by sniffing and circling around. The sniffing is to detect the smell of previous eliminations. These two aspects of behaviour are an aid in house training. First of all, as soon as the puppy shows signs that it is going to relieve itself, it should be picked up and carried outside to a chosen, convenient place in the garden. Once this has been used, it will be more likely to become acceptable as the odours remain. The puppy should be praised when it performs successfully in the correct place. Accidents are inevitable at this stage and, if they are witnessed or the evidence is discovered quickly, the puppy should be told off or smacked gently and taken to the proper place. It is not fair to rub its nose in the mess, as was sometimes advocated in the past. The puppy should be taken outside frequently during the day, particularly immediately after eating and on first waking up. It may be necessary to use newspapers at night at first, placed around the bed in a place with a floor that is easily cleaned. Any messes that are made in the house should be thoroughly cleaned up and the area disinfected. This removes odours that might encourage further lapses on the dog's part. As with all aspects of training, it is best to praise good behaviour and be relaxed and patient over mistakes. Most dogs learn clean habits fairly quickly, although individuals vary and some take longer than others.

Occasionally, an older dog that is already house-trained may urinate or defecate indoors. If this is a rare occurrence, it is likely to be because of some slight digestive upset or a result of over-eating or drinking. If the problem persists, veterinary advice should be sought in case there is a medical condition present that needs attention. Also, a dog may sometimes behave in this way because of anxiety and insecurity for which there may be some discernible cause, such as the arrival of a new baby or another dog.

Training courses and specialist training

In many towns and cities, there are dog training sessions run by a variety of organizations and ranging from basic to advanced. Your veterinary practice will usually be able to offer advice on where these are held in a particular locality. Both dog and owner attend the sessions, which are often held once a week, and they can be helpful for obtaining advice and reinforcing the training being carried out at home. More ambitious courses are available for suitable dogs and owners, and the results can be impressive.

ROUTINE CARE OF A DOG

Most aspects of caring for a dog on a day-to-day basis are a matter of common sense, although there are a few general points that should be noted. As has already been indicated, a puppy needs relatively more of its owner's attention than an older animal. A dog that is happy and settled in its home is capable of being quite flexible and fitting in with the family.

Walks and exercise

Some people worry about the amount of exercise needed by their dog and whether it is harmful for it to have either too much or too little. The amount of exercise required depends on the age, breed, size and state of health of the dog. Puppies and young dogs can be damaged by too much exercise before the age of six months, as joints and tendons may be stressed. Also, puppies should not be exercised, except in their own garden, until two weeks after routine vaccinations have been completed, as they are very vulnerable to infection at this stage. Any dog that has a history of hip problems should not be given too much exercise. This is particularly true for some of the larger breeds that may have a tendency to dislocation of the hip joints or hip displasia. All dogs are most active in young adult life, and many enjoy running about almost all the time without seeming to become unduly tired. For an active family or those who enjoy walking, this type of dog is a joy to have. It will always be eager to go out or ready to engage in a strenuous game with anyone who can be persuaded to play. Most dogs eventually become less active in old age and may suffer from arthritic, heart or other disorders that limit the amount of exercise needed. Old dogs will still enjoy the change and interest provided by a walk, but it may need to be of a shorter duration and taken at a slower pace than before. An old dog is more likely to appreciate two or more short walks rather than one long one. Obviously, if a dog has been ill or is recovering from surgery and has stitches in place, the amount of exercise should be reduced. Depending on its state of health, the animal may need only to be let out into the garden until it has recovered its strength.

In summary, active adult dogs with no health problems should have at least one hour's exercise each day, preferably including at least one walk with a good run off the lead. In addition, exercise can be provided by playing a 'throw and fetch' game with the dog and also by allowing it to accompany you while you are carrying out routine activities such as gardening. On a winter's day when the weather is cold and miserable and you still have to go for a walk, it may help to remember that a tired dog is more likely to be contented and sleep well at night. Even so, it will not matter if the walk has to be somewhat shorter than normal.

Grooming

All dogs should be groomed on a regular basis, preferably once each day, but frequency depends, to a certain extent, on the nature of the coat. Breeds with long or curly hair need grooming on a daily basis to deal with the tangles that inevitably form. A metal comb and a brush with long bristles that may be of natural materials, nylon or soft wire, are required for this purpose. A brush or grooming mitten is sufficient for short-haired and smooth-coated dogs, which are easier to deal with. Grooming helps to remove dead hairs, and this is particularly useful when the dog is moulting as it reduces the amount shed in the house. Brushing should be thorough to ensure that no areas of the body are missed out and, in general, follow the 'lie' of the coat. Any tangles that are encountered should be dealt with immediately and not left to get bigger. Small tangles can be prised apart with the fingers and then combed through, but if the fur has become very matted, perhaps with small twigs or other vegetation stuck in amongst the fur, it is best to cut these out with scissors. (When choosing a dog, it is worth remembering that the coat of a long-haired breed requires a great deal of attention to keep it in good order.) A puppy should become accustomed to grooming from an early age, by brushing regularly with an appropriate brush, so that it learns to accept this without a fuss. Daily brushing ensures that any thorns or seeds that might penetrate the skin and cause harm are more likely to be detected.

Some breeds require professional grooming in the form of clipping or stripping of the coat (although it is now possible to attend courses to acquire the necessary skills to carry this out at home). Breeds that need frequent clipping are usually those that do not moult, e.g. poodles, Kerry blue terriers and Bedlington terriers. However, several other breeds need occasional clipping, if only to reduce the weight and thickness of the coat in summer. These include the various types of spaniel, Old English sheepdog, keeshond, Newfoundland, Pomeranian, and others. In some breeds, dead hair needs to be stripped out of the coat using a special tool, and this is normally carried out about twice each year. Spaniels, wire-haired terriers and other thick-coated breeds may all benefit from regular stripping. Dog-grooming establishments are able to give a professional look to the long-haired, silky-coated breeds, and this is especially useful for owners who are short of time or when preparing for a show.

Bathing

All dogs benefit from an occasional bath but frequency depends on the individual dog and is largely a matter of personal choice. Obviously, it is desirable to bath a dog that has become filthy while out on a muddy walk or has rolled in something smelly before letting it into the house. The need is less great for a working sheepdog that is kept outside and frequently gets dirty, although this dog should also be given an occasional bath, preferably in the summer months when the weather is warm. The family bath or shower can be used or the dog can be bathed outside in a paddling pool, baby bath or using bowls and buckets. A shower attachment on the taps is particularly useful for rinsing all shampoo out of the coat. It is most important to use lukewarm water that feels neither too hot nor too cold. The dog should be placed in the water and the coat made thoroughly wet. Then a proprietary dog shampoo or mild family shampoo should be applied and worked into a lather. Great care must be taken in washing the head and, preferably, the ear canal should be protected with plugs of cotton wool. It may be best to use baby shampoo on the dog's head as this will not irritate the eyes and a squeezed-out sponge or flannel to wipe away most of the lather. Thorough rinsing is important to remove all traces of shampoo and, when the bath is finished, the dog should be wrapped in a large towel to soak up most of the moisture. It is preferable to do this before the dog has had time to shake itself although this will inevitably happen at some point. The dog should be dried as thoroughly as possible and kept in a warm place to avoid chilling. A hairdryer can be used as long as it is not placed too close to the dog and is moved continuously so that heat is not concentrated in one place.

It is important never to use human medicated shampoos or household detergents on a dog. Sometimes medicated or insecticidal preparations are necessary to treat a particular condition, but these should always be used in accordance with veterinary advice. If a dog develops any form of skin condition, veterinary help should be sought and home treatment should not be attempted. Some dogs, particularly spaniels, have oily coats because of an overproduction of a natural substance called sebum. These animals tend to develop an offensive 'doggy' smell and need to be bathed more frequently to keep this under control. In all dogs the use of shampoo removes natural oils from the coat and reduces its weather-resistant properties for a time. Hence it may be better not to bath a dog that is kept outdoors during very cold weather.

Paws and claws

A dog's paws are naturally vulnerable to cuts and abrasions and should be examined on a regular basis. Broken glass, mud, grit and tar, thorns and even seeds can all become embedded in or between the pads and cause harm. If this material penetrates the skin it can be responsible for boils or abscesses (see A-Z OF ILLNESSES, page 79), and this tends to be a problem in dogs that have deep crevices beneath the toes.

It may be necessary to clip the nails of a dog occasionally, although this very much depends on the individual animal and the amount of exercise it is receiving. Dogs getting plenty of exercise on hard ground, e.g. on gravel paths or pavements, usually have claws that are continually worn down and seldom require clipping. Country dogs exercised mainly in fields and woods or toy breeds receiving few walks may need to have their claws trimmed regularly. This is also the case with elderly or ill dogs, which are not able to have much exercise. If it is suspected that a dog's claws are becoming too long, it is best to take the animal to a veterinary surgeon in the first instance. It is perfectly possible to learn how to trim the claws correctly, using clippers designed for the purpose so that it can be carried out at home in the future. The main point to remember is that there can be considerable bleeding if too much of the nail is taken off and the 'quick', which contains blood vessels, is severed. When trimming a dog's nails at home it is best to cut a little more frequently rather than too much all at once. Also, the dog may object to the whole process, and this is especially likely to happen if you inadvertently cause pain and bleeding. The claws that are most likely to grow too long are the 'dew claws', which occur on the 'thumbs' of the dog. These are located a few inches above the foot on the inner side of the leg. They may be present only on the front legs but sometimes on the back ones too. Since they never come into contact with the ground they are not worn down naturally and may eventually become too long. In some puppies the dew claws are removed shortly after birth but if present, their length should be monitored and clipping carried out if needed.

Cleaning teeth

Dental problems in dogs result from a build-up of tartar or calculus on the teeth. This occurs in the presence of bacterial growth, plaque or accumulations of trapped food and naturally-occurring salts precipitated from the dog's saliva. Teeth most affected by plaque are the canines, premolars and molars, and the build-up generally occurs at the junction of teeth and gums. Eventually, if the accumulation continues unchecked, periodontal disease, with infected painful gums and loose teeth, may result. Dogs that eat a diet containing hard or dried foods or that regularly use their teeth for chewing toys, chews or bones normally have very little tartar. Problems arise in those that eat soft foods and do not use their teeth in other ways. Toy breeds are especially prone to periodontal disease, but in all dogs it is advisable to prevent the build-up of tartar. In addition to providing hard foods or toys for chewing, regular brushing with a specially designed dog toothbrush and toothpaste is advisable. It is better to do this once a day but once a week may be sufficient. Obviously it is easier if the dog does not object and many get used to this procedure eventually, particularly if it is started at a time when there are no dental problems.

Care of the ears

The ears can be a common site for problems and should be examined regularly. Dogs most likely to be affected are those with long, floppy ears, such as spaniels, probably because air cannot circulate very easily. Dogs that do not shed hair, such as poodles, need to have this clipped from the outer part of the ear. Occasionally it may be necessary to clean the ears if there is a build-up of wax or other debris. This can be carried out at home using lukewarm liquid paraffin or other oil, as advised by a veterinary surgeon. If a dog has any sign of irritation, inflammation or discharge, often obvious because the animal tends to shake its head, hold it on one side or paw at its ear, it requires prompt veterinary attention. There may be a foreign body such as a grass seed or other particle lodged in the ear, a bacterial infection or the presence of ear mites (*see* PARASITES, page 74). All these conditions should be dealt with by a veterinary surgeon and require a particular course of treatment to be followed.

Eye care

Dogs' eyes differ from those of humans in several ways. Firstly, they possess a third eyelid, called a nictitating membrane or haw, which is located in the inner corner of each eye. This can be easily seen in some breeds, e.g. spaniels and bloodhounds, and may become prominent and protrude in a dog that is severely dehydrated. The position of the eyes on the head give the dog a greater field of vision than humans. Dogs have many more rod cells in the retina of the eye, which give them sharper vision in poor light. However, they have fewer cone cells and poorer colour vision than humans. A dog's eyes are very good at detecting movement, although they do not perceive static objects in the immediate vicinity so accurately. In common with many other mammals, a layer called the *tapetum lucidum* is present behind the retina, which reflects light back and intensifies an image. This can be clearly seen if a light is shone into the eyes at night when they appear to glow a greenish-yellow colour.

In general, a dog's eyes do not require any care at home. If a problem arises such as obvious inflammation or irritation, with watering and holding the eye shut, the dog should be treated by a veterinary surgeon. Occasionally a little dry material may crust in the corner of an eye. This can be removed using clean, moist cotton wool, wiping in one direction from the corner of the eye outwards. Some white or light-coloured dogs, such as poodles, Maltese and Bedlington terriers, Pekinese and pugs, tend to have an overflow of 'tears' down the face, producing a characteristic brownish line. Preparations to remove the staining are available for external use on the dog's face. A more successful treatment, however, is a course of the antibiotic tetracycline. This neutralizes substances called porphyrins that are present in the tears and are responsible for the brown stains.

Worming

Responsible ownership involves regular dosing with medication designed to eliminate the two types of internal parasite that are common in dogs, roundworms and tapeworms. A great variety of de-worming preparations are available in the form of tablets, syrups or creams. Some act solely on one type of worm while others are combined preparations that will eliminate both. Particular vigilance is necessary to control roundworms in bitches before and after they give birth, and in puppies. It is wise to consult a veterinary surgeon who will advise on the type of preparation needed for any particular dog and on frequency of use. (*See* LABOUR AND BIRTH, page 60; PARASITES, page 65.)

Vaccination

It is vitally important to protect the health of a puppy or older dog by making sure it is vaccinated against certain serious diseases that can prove fatal in untreated animals. Routine vaccination provides protection against the following infections:
—distemper or hardpad, a viral disease
—infectious canine hepatitis, a viral disease (canine adenovirus)
—leptospirosis, two bacterial infections, each caused by a different
   strain of micro-organism

—parvovirus, a viral disease of the respiratory tract
—parainfluenza, a viral disease of the respiratory tract

After birth and while suckling, puppies receive some natural antibodies from their mother in the colostrum. The most effective time to start the course of vaccination is when the puppy is about eight to twelve weeks of age when this natural immunity has declined. If a dog has been acquired from a rescue or welfare centre, it is fairly certain not to have been vaccinated and it should be protected in the same way. A puppy should not normally be vaccinated before the recommended age, unless a veterinary surgeon considers it to be at particular risk as a result of certain special circumstances. This is because if antibodies derived from the mother are still present they can render the vaccine less effective and diminish immunity.

Following the first dose, a second vaccination injection is given four weeks later. Before it has been vaccinated, and for the two weeks following the final injection, the puppy or dog should be kept away from other dogs. It should also be kept away from areas where other dogs are exercised as the ground is a potential source of infection. After completion of the initial course, a yearly booster vaccination is needed. Certain other diseases occur against which vaccination can be given if needed. These include kennel cough, rabies and tetanus (*see* A-Z OF ILLNESSES, pages 116, 129 and 136).

Leaving your dog—boarding kennels

Some owners worry considerably about how their dog will adjust if it has to be left with other people while they are away. Obviously, it is more pleasant for the dog if it can be left with a friend or relative whom it knows well and who can provide a 'home from home'. Depending on individual temperament, some dogs will be perfectly happy with this arrangement while others may fret a little at first but will usually soon settle down. However, if this is not possible the dog will need to be housed in boarding kennels. In most areas, there are plenty of boarding kennels, and it is often helpful to ask around to see if one is particularly recommended. Entries in the telephone directory also give a useful clue as to the type of service provided. Naturally, it is a good idea to visit the kennels yourself, well in advance of your departure, so that you can form an opinion as to how well run they are. All reputable kennels will welcome and even expect such a visit, and it is a case of trusting your own judgement—if you like the look of the place and the owners, then you will feel happy about leaving your dog there. It is worth bearing in mind that boarding kennels become booked up very quickly in school holidays so it is necessary to make plans well in advance to be sure of securing a place. Also, most require that dogs boarded on their premises are up-to-date with vaccinations (*see* page 41) and may wish to see the certificate. Some may insist that dogs are vaccinated against kennel cough (*see* page 116), so it is wise to ensure that you have fulfilled all the necessary requirements.

If, on acquiring a dog, you know that you will need to use kennels on a regular basis, it is best to introduce this quite early on once the animal has settled down with you. Some kennels will keep a dog just for the day. This is an ideal way of getting the dog used to the idea that when it is left there it has not been abandoned and that you will return to take it home. Many dogs learn to accept a stay in kennels, even if they do not enjoy it very much, and will always be ecstatic about going home. Some may fret a little or go off their food. but kennel owners are usually prepared to do a great deal to reassure an unhappy dog and to coax it to eat. Most dogs will not come to any harm if they lose a little weight. Some dogs show their insecurity by barking themselves hoarse, and there is little that can be done about this. The dog will normally soon recover its 'voice' once it has returned home. If you are concerned that your dog may feel anxious in kennels, there are one or two things that can be done that may help. The dog can have its own bed, blankets and toy to remind it of home, and you can make sure that the type of food offered is the type the animal is used to. Most kennel owners are happy to comply with reasonable requests that will help an individual dog to settle down more easily.

Often, it is the owners who experience more anxiety about their pet than the dog itself. It has to be said, however, that some dogs are very unhappy about being left in kennels, and this can cause problems. This is more likely to be the case with an older dog that has not been used to anything other than its own home.

INSURANCE

The cost of veterinary treatment for a dog that has been injured, or needs prolonged or intensive care during an illness, can be quite considerable. Also, if a dog damages other people's property or livestock or causes an accident, its owner may be liable for the payment of hefty damages. It is well worth considering taking out an insurance policy to cover these potential costs rather than suddenly to be faced with a large bill. Obviously, this is a matter of personal choice and, at the present time, relatively few dog owners insure their pets in this way. Insurance can be money well spent and bring peace of mind, particularly with regard to the cost of veterinary treatment. It may save an owner from a great deal of heartache as it is impossible to predict whether any particular dog may, at some stage, need expensive treatment.

SEXUAL BEHAVIOUR AND BREEDING

Male dog

Male dogs usually reach sexual maturity or puberty between the ages of six to twelve months, although this varies somewhat among different breeds and individuals. Most dogs reach puberty later than the corresponding bitches of that breed, although in some this occurs earlier. Male puppies practise sexual behaviour, in the form of mounting and pelvic thrusting, as part of their early repertoire of play. Most lose this behaviour as they go through puberty and into adulthood. Sexual behaviour is then normally triggered if the dog gains access to a bitch on heat.

The testicles of the male puppy are formed within the abdomen during the development of the embryo. The testicles normally descend via the inguinal canal into a pocket or pouch called the scrotum, attached to the underside of the body between the hind legs. The testicles are usually in place by the time the puppy is born, but in some dogs the final descent occurs during the first few days after birth. In some dogs, as in humans, a testicle can retract and descend again during the early weeks after birth. Occasionally, one or both testicles may fail to descend and this condition is called cryptorchidism. Usually only one fails to come down (monorchidism), and it is usually the right testicle that does not descend. A dog that has one retained testicle is still fertile and capable of breeding. Since this condition tends to be inherited, however, such a dog should not be used for breeding and is not able to enter official shows. In humans, a surgical procedure can be performed to bring down an undescended testicle and hold it in its proper place in the scrotal sac. This operation is not performed on dogs as it could not correct the fact that this is an inherited disorder and the animal would still be ineligible for breeding. In dogs as well as humans, there is a significantly increased risk of a retained testicle becoming cancerous at a later stage. A dog with this condition must therefore undergo an operation to remove the retained testicle. In fact, the normal course of treatment for a male dog with this condition is surgical removal of both testicles, including the one that is not retained (castration), to prevent any possibility of breeding and passing on the defective gene.

Male dogs, in common with a number of other mammals including cats, have a bone in the penis called the os penis or baculum. This is a narrow bone that is broader at the end nearest the body and tapers towards the outside. It has a groove along its length in which lies a tube, called the urethra, that conveys urine from the bladder to the outside. The function of the bone is almost certainly to help maintain the rigidity of the penis during mating.

Having reached puberty, all male dogs are normally very attracted to any bitch in the vicinity that is sexually receptive ('in season' or 'oestrus' or 'on heat'). The bitch produces powerful chemical substances called sex pheromones, which are irresistible to males. So strong is the urge to mate that the dog may forget its training and love of its home and wander away to sit on the doorstep of the home of the bitch. If wandering is persistent, and it proves difficult to keep the dog confined, or it strays while out on a walk, castration is one approach that can be considered (*see* page 120). This successfully reduces the behaviour in about 90–95 per cent of male dogs. Another option is the administration of synthetic hormonal substances, called progestagens, which may prove to be effective. A veterinary surgeon will be happy to give advice and recommend suitable treatment and, in general, a responsible owner should take steps to ensure that a male dog does not become a father. This will help to reduce the vast numbers of unwanted dogs that are such a problem for animal rescue and welfare centres. Of course, some pedigree males are highly valued as stud dogs for breeding. Such a dog should not, however, be allowed to mate before the age of ten months to one year. He should be at least two years old before he is used for breeding on a regular basis. A stud dog should be maintained at the correct weight and not allowed to become fat, and he should be given plenty of exercise to keep him fit but does not need any other special care.

A dog shows his interest in a bitch on heat by licking and sniffing at her genital area. If the bitch is ready to mate and willing to accept the dog, she stands still and holds her tail up and to one side. The dog mounts by rearing on to his hind legs and clasping the bitch with his front ones around her abdomen. The penis is introduced into the vagina and the dog begins a number of thrusting movements. This causes the bulbous end of the penis to enlarge, and at the same time muscles in the wall of the vagina of the bitch contract so that the two animals become 'tied' or 'locked' together. It is not possible to separate the dog and bitch once this has taken place, and it should never be attempted even if the mating is an unscheduled one but should be allowed to take its natural course. In a few breeds, however, such as the chow-chow, successful mating occurs without the male and female becoming tied so this presumably is not essential. Action can be taken afterwards to prevent a bitch from becoming pregnant, if necessary.

The male dog ejaculates sperm after the pelvic thrusts have finished and then drops down with his front feet to one side of the bitch. He then raises a hind leg over her back and turns so that the two are tied with their rear quarters together and their heads at opposite ends. The female may pull against the tie, but this usually lasts for an average of three-quarters of an hour, although it may be shorter or longer. During this stage, fluid from the prostate gland of the male is released into the female's reproductive tract. Eventually, the tie is broken when the penis of the male decreases in size and the vaginal muscles of the bitch relax. The two animals normally part and each lies down and licks its genital organs for some time after the mating. Since the whole process is quite a lengthy one, a male dog is capable of only a few matings in any particular day and should not be expected to perform too frequently. The best and most usual procedure is to bring the bitch to the dog to be mated so that the dog is in its familiar home surroundings. The male dog does not have a breeding season as such and is able to mate throughout the year, although there are likely to be peaks and troughs in its libido.

Bitch

A female puppy or bitch reaches sexual maturity or puberty at roughly the same age as a male, i.e. on average between six to twelve months old. There is, however, a great deal of variation in individual animals and among the different breeds. In general, bitches belonging to little breeds and smaller mongrels or cross-breeds reach puberty at a younger age than larger animals. In the bitch, puberty is marked by the animal coming 'on heat' or 'in season' for the first time. In common with all female mammals, bitches undergo reproductive cycles called oestrous cycles, which regulate when they are able to mate and give birth to young. These are triggered by the release of hormones within the body and are ultimately controlled by a special centre in the brain called the hypothalamus.

Unlike the situation in many other mammals, oestrous cycles do not seem to be dependent upon seasonal or climatic factors in dogs. In between each oestrous cycle there is a quiescent inter-oestrous or anoestrous period when the bitch is not sexually active or capable of breeding. In general terms, most bitches have at least one oestrous cycle each year with inter-oestrous lasting, on average, for about seven to eight months. However, there is an enormous amount of variation in this, both among the different breeds, in bitches of the same breed and even in the life of an individual dog. The start of the oestrous cycle is known as the pro-oestrous stage, and it may last from four to thirteen days, with nine being the usual average. In pro-oestrous the external genital organs or vulva become engorged and reddened and there is a blood-stained dis-

charge. The blood originates in the vagina and may be noticed as
spotting on the animal's bed or on carpets and furnishings in the
home. (It may be necessary to prevent soiling by making sure that
the bitch sits or lies only in her own bed, or on an old rug or towel,
while she is going through this stage.) Most bitches lick and clean
themselves quite thoroughly and so spotting should only be slight.
Some people make the mistake of equating this bleeding with menstruation in human females, although the two situations are entirely
dissimilar. In the bitch, the bleeding occurs at the start of the fertile
period *before* the release of eggs (ovulation) takes place and prior
to mating and possible pregnancy. Conversely, menstruation occurs *after* ovulation, when an egg has been shed but neither fertilized nor implanted in the womb, and so pregnancy has not taken
place. It is quite common for a bitch to be unsettled at this stage
and she may urinate more often than is normal.

In the pre-oestrus stage, the bitch's behaviour changes and she
becomes more interested in male dogs, although she rebuffs any attempts at mating. The next period in the cycle is the oestrous stage,
and it normally lasts for about nine days although, once again, it
may be shorter or longer. It is during this stage that the bitch per-
mits mating with selected males. The blood-stained discharge becomes clear during the oestrous stage and contains the potent
chemical messengers, known as sexual pheromones, that are irre-
sistibly attractive to male dogs. One pheromone in particular, me-
thyl P-hydroxybenzoate, seems to be responsible for stimulating
the male to mount the bitch and mate. Ovulation or release of eggs
generally occurs at the beginning of the oestrous period and, also at
this time, pheromone release is at its strongest. The bitch is now at
her most receptive and fertile and is driven by the urge to mate.
Like the male, a bitch may wander or run away at this stage and
will usually mate with a dog that the owner considers unsuitable.
Also, a bitch may mate with several males during the oestrous period, so it is possible for eggs to be fertilized by separate males and
for the same litter of puppies to have different fathers. This is
called superfecundation. As the oestrous period progresses,
pheromone release and fertility decline gradually and the animal
either enters the anoestrous or inter-oestrous phase or has become

pregnant. A further phenomenon that may follow a heat period is false or pseudo-pregnancy (*see* page 50).

It can be seen from the above that it is better to avoid unplanned matings. One approach is to keep the bitch confined to her own home and garden as long as it is certain that the premises are adequately fenced and 'dog-proof'. Various deodorant preparations are available to mask the pheromones produced during heat. Also, hormonal contraceptive preparations can be given, either to delay a period of heat or to suppress it once it has started. These can be administered only by a veterinary surgeon and may either be in the form of tablets or injections. They are generally advisable only for bitches that may be used for breeding at some stage but are presently at risk of an unwanted pregnancy. If the intention is never to allow a bitch to have puppies, usually the best option is to have her spayed or neutered (*see* page 120). A bitch should have her first litter of puppies before the age of four or five years. This is because in a young dog there is fibrous connective tissue joining the two halves of the pelvic bone, which has some degree of flexibility. At whelping this 'gives', so the bones to move apart, allowing easier passage for each puppy's head. In an older dog, the fibrous material gradually becomes rigid as it is changed into bone. Hence in an older bitch there is likely to be more difficulty in the process of labour and birth, especially in those breeds that produce puppies with larger heads. A breeding bitch should not be used for this purpose after eight years old because of the changes that occur in bone structure and the general stress of pregnancy. For these reasons, during the time that she is used for breeding, she should not be allowed to have more than one litter each year. The first litter should ideally be produced at the age of about one and a half years, when the bitch has stopped growing. Producing a litter early on interrupts the maturing process and places a great deal of stress on a young dog.

If a bitch has got out and it is suspected that an unscheduled mating may have taken place, pregnancy can be prevented by giving the hormone oestrogen. This is in the form of an injection that must be given within 48 hours of a possible mating and is administered by a veterinary surgeon. Oestrogen has the effect of extending the heat period so extra care must be exercised during this time. There is also a higher than normal risk of the bitch developing an infection of the womb, a condition known as pyometra (*see* page 128).

False or pseudo-pregnancy (phantom pregnancy or pseudo-cyesis)

Following a period of heat, it is not unusual for a bitch that has not been mated to develop signs of pregnancy. These signs include both physical and behavioural changes and vary from slight to quite intense. Physical manifestations include enlargement of the uterus and abdomen, even although no embryos are growing in the womb, and swelling of the milk-producing mammary glands. These may even start to produce milk and some bitches suckle themselves, so perpetuating milk production. The bitch may act as though she is preparing for whelping by becoming restless or anxious and showing nesting behaviour. The reason for these changes is the release of the natural hormone progesterone within the body. After ovulation, a structure called the corpus luteum develops on the outside of the ovary at the place from which an egg was released. Several corpora lutea develop in the bitch, depending on the number of eggs that were shed. Each corpus luteum produces progesterone, and if eggs are fertilized by mating, this hormone is responsible for their successful implantation into the womb and for the maintenance of the pregnancy. In most mammals, if the eggs are not fertilized and there is no pregnancy, the corpora lutea degenerate and cease to produce progesterone. However, in the bitch they are more long-lasting and continue to produce progesterone, so causing the signs of phantom pregnancy. Pseudo-pregnancy can persist for a month or even longer and, provided that the symptoms are not pronounced, there is no need to take any action. Providing the dog with plenty of exercise and attention will help to tire her out and divert her from her condition. If the symptoms are pronounced or the condition is a recurrent one, a veterinary surgeon should be consulted. If the bitch is not going to be needed for breeding, the best option is to have her spayed or neutered (*see* page 120). Allowing the animal to have one litter of puppies does not alleviate subsequent symptoms of pseudo-pregnancy since these are triggered by hormonal factors.

Planned mating of a bitch

Those wishing to breed a litter of puppies from a bitch must first locate a suitable stud dog and arrange for a mating. The various associations, and publications connected with dogs and the Kennel Club are all useful sources of information. Local veterinary practices may know if a stud dog of the required breed can be found in the area, or the original breeder of the bitch may be able to help. It is the usual procedure for the bitch to be taken to the home of the stud dog and ten days from the onset of the heat period is considered to be the optimum time for mating. This can be difficult to calculate with accuracy and sometimes the bitch remains at the home of the dog for a few days so that there is a greater chance of a successful mating.

Pregnancy

The average length of gestation or pregnancy in dogs is about 63 days, although it may vary between a few days on either side, depending on the breed. In dogs, the womb or uterus consists of a short 'body' and two comparatively long 'horns' that each connect at the outer end with an ovary via a tube called the oviduct. Hence the womb is shaped somewhat like the letter Y. After mating and fertilization, the eggs travel down the oviducts to settle in the horns (arms of the Y) of the womb where they subsequently develop.

The first phase of pregnancy, known as the 'period of the egg', lasts for nineteen days in dogs. Usually there are a number of eggs that are distributed at regular intervals along the length of each horn. They are not attached at this stage but bathed and nourished by fluid in the womb.

The second phase of pregnancy is called the 'period of the embryo'. During this stage, each embryo becomes surrounded by a placenta, and this is a period of rapid development when major tissues and organs are formed. It lasts from the twentieth to the thirty-third day.

The final phase is called the 'period of the foetus' and is the stage of major growth during which the puppies become fully formed and ready for birth.

In the first three to four weeks there is little outward sign of pregnancy and the bitch should continue to receive her normal diet. At around three and a half weeks, a veterinary surgeon will normally be able to detect the pregnancy by carefully feeling the abdomen of the bitch. The embryos at this stage are rather like small round pebbles but may be damaged by inexpert handling. From about four to seven weeks, the developing foetuses are cushioned by protective fluid and cannot be felt externally. However, at around this stage of five weeks onwards, the abdomen of the bitch starts to enlarge noticeably as the puppies are developing very rapidly. Also, at about five weeks, the milk or mammary glands become larger and the teats more protuberant. The skin may become a brighter pink and there may be a discharge of fluid or even milk from the teats a few days before the birth. A bitch having her first litter does not usually produce true milk until after the birth. With subsequent litters milk may be discharged before the puppies are born. Changes in colour and size of the mammary glands and teats are also more noticeable in a bitch having her first litter.

After the first month, the bitch will require more food to cope with the demands being placed on her body. She should receive up to half as much again on top of her normal ration in the form of high quality protein food. It is best to feed several small meals a day, as the stomach becomes restricted because of the expansion of the womb. Obviously, overall weight gain during pregnancy varies according to the size and breed of dog and the number of puppies being carried. It may be anything from 1–7 kg (2–16 lbs) and the number of puppies varies between one and fourteen. It is wise to consult a veterinary surgeon if there are any doubts about care during pregnancy. About one month before the birth the bitch should be treated for roundworms (*see* page 66), and this is normally repeated during the period when she is suckling to reduce infestation in the puppies. A veterinary surgeon will advise about the preparation to use and also whether any booster vaccinations are necessary. Some dogs become constipated towards the end of pregnancy, and this can be eased by giving a laxative, as advised by the veterinary surgeon. A healthy pregnant bitch should continue to receive her daily walks in order to keep muscles toned and to prevent obesity. Vigorous activity, especially jumping, should be discouraged.

By the end of the pregnancy the dog will probably feel too heavy and lethargic to bother with too much running about.

Preparing for the birth of puppies

The most important preparation to be made is to provide the bitch with a warm, comfortable and quiet place in which to have her puppies. Her usual bed may not be suitable for the purpose as it has to accommodate both the bitch and a growing litter of puppies. For small dogs, a strong thick cardboard box lined with plenty of newspaper and with the front cut down is quite adequate. It may be necessary to buy or construct a wooden whelping box especially designed for the purpose. This is a shallow wooden box, but with sides high enough to keep out draughts, i.e. at least 15 cm (6 ins) in height, raised off the ground on legs or runners. The front of the box is often hinged so that it can be let down or may have a similar central 'doorway'. A shallow ledge about 7.5 cm (3 ins) wide is attached to the three fixed sides of the box. This forms a narrow shelf that is constructed about 5 to 7.5 cm (2 to 3 ins) above the base of the box. Its purpose is to prevent the bitch from accidentally crushing a new-born puppy against the side of the box when she lies down, as it keeps her away from the edge. The box should be placed in a quiet, secure place that is maintained at a constant temperature of about 27°C (80°F) once the puppies are born. It may be necessary to provide some form of screen to keep out draughts, and a suspended heat lamp can be useful in making sure that it is warm enough. The bitch should be introduced to the box at least two weeks before the expected time of whelping so that she learns to accept the new sleeping arrangements.

Often a bitch has been seen by a veterinary surgeon at some stage during the pregnancy. If this is not the case, however, it is advisable to make sure that the veterinary practice is aware of the expected date of whelping in case expert help is needed. In a long-haired dog, it may be a good idea to clip the area around the vulva and teats if this can be carried out without causing distress. Other advance preparations include:

1 setting aside a few clean towels for drying the new-born puppies (if the bitch fails to lick them);

2 having ready a pair of scissors and some strong thread, which have been sterilized by boiling or immersion in a proprietary solution. These may be required for tying off and cutting an umbilical cord;

3 making sure you have a hot-water bottle with a protective cover to hand. A first puppy can be placed on or near this to keep warm while other puppies are being born;

4 setting aside a bowl, towel and soap for washing hands in the event of having to handle the puppies during or after birth.

All these items should be placed in a convenient place close to the whelping box so that it is not necessary to hunt around for them in the middle of the night.

Behaviour of the bitch just before giving birth

Most bitches show some signs to indicate that the birth of the puppies is imminent. These include whining and restlessness and an inability to settle. A few days before the birth, there may be a secretion of milk from the teats of a bitch that has had puppies before, or a clear fluid in the case of one giving birth for the first time.

LABOUR AND BIRTH

During the last twenty-four hours before giving birth, which can be equated with the first stage of labour, the restlessness of the bitch becomes increasingly marked. Usually she visits the whelping box (or other chosen spot) frequently and tears up the bedding and carries it about to create a suitable nest. The entrance to the vagina or vulva becomes more prominent, producing a clear discharge, and the bitch usually licks and cleans this area quite thoroughly. If the temperature is taken, it will be seen to have fallen from a normal of 37.8–38.6°C (100°–101.5°F) to 36.67–37.5°C (98°–99.5°F). The animal often refuses food and drink, and it is advisable to make sure that she goes outside to relieve herself. The bitch should be allowed to remain near her box without undue interference and noise. Some contractions of the womb are taking place during this stage, and although these cannot be detected externally, they may be indicated by trembling and panting.

During the second stage of labour, uterine contractions become strong, visible and regular, and may cause distress. The bitch may cry out, pant or moan, but usually after about one hour, the first puppy, surrounded by its protective fluid-filled membrane, is visible at the vulva. The sac may burst, with a gush of clear fluid, during the passage down the birth canal but, if intact, is a dull greyish colour. Most puppies are born in one of two common positions. The first position, which is usually called normal presentation, is when the head is delivered first. The top of the puppy's head and the surface of its back are uppermost and its nose is pointed downwards. The second position is when the hind legs and then the rear end of the puppy are delivered first, followed by the head. About one-third to a half of all puppies present in one of these positions. A breech birth occurs when the tail and rear end of the puppy are born first but with the hind legs tucked up beneath the belly. In a bitch having puppies for the first time, the birth of the first may cause considerable pain, with forceful contractions and straining. Most bitches lie down but others may stand for some of the time. The puppy is usually born either completely or partially surrounded by the amniotic membrane, which will still contain fluid if this has not ruptured previously.

Immediately the puppy is born the bitch usually licks it thoroughly and bites through the membrane and umbilical cord attaching it to the placenta. The vigorous licking of the mother stimulates the puppy to breathe, and it very soon makes its way to the bitch's teats. Within the next five minutes to a quarter of an hour, the contractions generally resume and the placenta or afterbirth is expelled, marking the third stage of labour. The placenta is a deep colour, and it is normal for some dark green fluid to be passed and a little blood. The bitch usually eats the placenta, membrane and cord, and no attempt should be made to prevent this. It is believed to be a natural instinct common to many mammals in order, perhaps, to conceal the evidence of birth from potential predators as soon as possible. After the birth of the first puppy, the bitch may be very tired and may rest or sleep before contractions start up again to deliver the next one. The usual interval between puppies varies from about a quarter of an hour to an hour and sometimes even longer. It is most important to count the number of placentas and make sure that one is expelled for each puppy that is born. A retained placenta is likely later to cause a uterine infection and potentially serious systemic (whole body) illness in the bitch. A placenta is not necessarily expelled soon after the birth of the puppy. It may come out with the next pup, or two or three placentas may even be expelled together. The most effective way of ensuring sure that all are accounted for is to count them, particularly in the case of a large litter of puppies.

Depending on the number of puppies, the whole delivery process may take between two and ten hours. When all are born, contractions stop and the bitch finally settles down to rest and suckle the puppies. She should be given the opportunity to go outside and offered food and drink. The bitch will obviously be reluctant to leave her new pups but if she consents to do this for a moment, any soiled newspaper can be quickly replaced.

When to intervene or call a vet

In general, a bitch manages the birth quite well on her own, and if it is evident that all is proceeding smoothly, she should be left in peace but kept under unobtrusive observation. There are occasions, however, when it may be necessary to give some assistance or to call for expert veterinary help. You should intervene in the following circumstances:

1 the puppy is in one of the two common birth positions (i.e. head first or hind legs first) and is partly outside but there is difficulty in delivering the rest of the body. This is indicated by strong contractions and straining but the puppy does not move outwards and may even slip back a little when the bitch's body relaxes. Take a firm but gentle hold on the puppy, using a piece of clean towel. When a contraction begins, pull steadily downwards and outwards. When the contraction finishes, you should try to hold the puppy in the new position that has been achieved and not let it slip back again. All being well, the puppy will be delivered with this additional assistance but, if not, it is necessary to call immediately for veterinary help.

2 the puppy is born still enclosed in its fluid-filled amniotic mem-

brane and the bitch fails to bite through this and the umbilical cord. Using the fingers or a sterile pair of scissors, the membrane should be punctured close to the puppy's mouth to enable it to breathe. The puppy can be returned to the mother to see if she will now lick it to encourage breathing and movement and pull away the membrane. If this does not occur, the membrane can be removed with the fingers and the puppy dried with a towel. The umbilical cord needs to be severed if the bitch fails to bite through this herself. It should be tied with sterile thread about 5 cm (2 ins) from the puppy's body. It can then be cut with sterilized scissors on the outer side of the knot away from the body and the puppy may then be returned to its mother.

3 a puppy appears to be cold and blue, is not breathing and seems lifeless. In these circumstances, the puppy should be wrapped in a warm towel and its mouth opened. The tongue should be pulled gently forwards with the fingers so that the airway is not obstructed. Next, air should be blown into the puppy's mouth, directing the flow towards the throat. There is no need for direct contact between your mouth and the puppy's. At the same time, if possible, the puppy's body should be rubbed with the towel to help to stimulate breathing movements. A puppy can survive a fairly prolonged period of lack of oxygen, and it is worth persevering to try to revive one that is apparently lifeless.

You should call for veterinary assistance if any of the following occur either during or soon after birth:

1 the puppy is obviously stuck or there is an abnormal, transverse presentation. In this case, an emergency caesarean operation may be required and help is needed as soon as possible.

2 you have reason to suspect that a placenta may have been retained.

3 any puppy appears to be distressed in any way or is abnormal or deformed.

4 the bitch has had strong contractions but a puppy fails to be born after a reasonable time. The contractions may cease or the bitch may become exhausted after straining for a considerable time. These circumstances can arise at any stage during the delivery of the litter, and the condition is known as uterine inertia. An injec-

tion to restart contractions may be required or the puppies may
need to be delivered by caesarean section.

5 there is a foul-smelling discharge at any stage before, during or
after the birth of the puppies. This may indicate a number of situations, including the presence of an infection, a retained placenta
or an unborn puppy that has died. All these are potentially dangerous for the bitch and require investigation and treatment. It
should be noted that it is normal for the bitch to produce a reddish discharge for one or two weeks following birth.

6 the bitch appears ill in any way following the birth. One condition that may occur is mastitis, or inflammation of the mammary
glands. One or more glands becomes hot, swollen and painful, and
the bitch will not allow the puppies to feed. Later on, the
teats may become sore because of the demands of the puppies,
especially once they develop sharp milk teeth at the age of about
three weeks. Another life-threatening illness that can occur in the
bitch is eclampsia, or 'milk fever'. It is caused by a depletion of
calcium in the blood as a result of the considerable amounts that
are needed during development of the puppies for formation of
bones and teeth, and also for milk production in the first few
weeks. The illness can have a rapid onset, and symptoms include
restlessness and whining, lack of interest in the puppies, lethargy, unsteadiness and stiffness in walking, and eventually muscular spasms and convulsions. Treatment by an injection of calcium is needed immediately and usually results in a dramatic improvement. Prevention includes making sure that the bitch is fed
a good diet containing plenty of calcium both during pregnancy
and lactation. It is not recommended, however, that calcium supplements should be given. Eclampsia usually occurs in smaller
bitches, particularly if the litter of puppies is a large one.

Routine care of the bitch and puppies

Once all the puppies are born, the bitch should be offered food and
drink and, as mentioned previously, given the opportunity to go
outside if she can be coaxed into doing so. A bitch is usually very
protective of her puppies during the first few days and is reluctant
to leave them even for a short time of time. She looks after all their

needs for the first three weeks by suckling and licking them, and cleaning up waste that is passed. The demands on the bitch's body are very considerable and increase as the puppies rapidly grow. Hence she should be offered proportionately more food of a high nutritional value. This should be given as several meals a day, and there is no harm in offering as much as the bitch wants to eat at this time. The amount can be gradually reduced as the puppies go through weaning until the bitch is receiving her normal diet once this process is completed. The bitch should be treated for round-worms during the period when she is feeding the puppies. A veterinary surgeon can advise on the timing of this and the best preparation to use.

A new-born puppy appears to be very helpless and the eyes remain shut for the first two weeks. However, it is 'programmed' to crawl towards and locate its mother's teats and will normally suckle soon after birth, once it has been licked and cleaned. Suckling is interrupted while each member of the litter is born, and it may be necessary to remove early puppies to a warm place until birth is complete. In the first few days, the puppies spend all their time suckling or sleeping, and it is important that each receives the first milk, or colostrum, that gives immunity against disease. Puppies feed frequently at the start, but the time between suckling gradually increases as they grow and are able to take in more milk at each feed. During suckling, each puppy presses around the teat with its front legs while the hind ones work to push it closer to the bitch's body. This may stimulate the flow of milk. The eyes open after about two weeks and the puppy becomes more proficient at crawling, so that by three weeks of age it can stand and is able to move both forwards and backwards. Up until this age, the puppy eliminates waste when stimulated to do so by the licking of its mother. From the age of three weeks, however, this activity is under the control of the brain of the puppy rather than being an involuntary action.

At this age the puppy starts to become more adventurous and weaning can begin. The sense of hearing develops, and by the age of four weeks the puppy is able to detect accurately the direction of a sound. Also, at around three weeks of age, a puppy's sharp milk teeth erupt. Puppies may nip their mother's teats during suckling, making them quite sore. This usually coincides with the period when the bitch starts to become less protective towards her puppies, reducing the time spent with them and limiting suckling. She also rebukes them if they misbehave, and by the time the puppies are six weeks old will probably spend only a little time with them, with suckling reduced to a minimum. During the period of three to eight weeks, when the bitch becomes more relaxed about motherhood, it is important that the puppies' experiences and contact with people are widened. This means that they will be well prepared when they go to new homes at around the age of eight weeks. Young puppies are at risk from roundworm infestation (*see* page 66) and can become quite ill. They therefore need to be treated for this at regular intervals, usually starting at the age of about two weeks and continuing until they are four months old, with the bitch being dosed at the same time. It is important to be vigilant about this and to maintain standards of hygiene, especially making sure that children wash their hands and scrub beneath their nails after handling puppies or playing on ground that could be contaminated with worm eggs.

At the time of weaning some bitches regurgitate their food in the manner of wild dogs. To prevent this the bitch should be fed away from the puppies and perhaps taken for a walk or kept apart from them for some time. If the milk supply fails to dry up as weaning progresses, a veterinary surgeon should be consulted as some medication may be needed to deal with this problem.

In summary, interference with the bitch and her puppies should be kept to a minimum during the first three weeks, other than making sure that they are kept warm, soiled bedding is replaced and worming attended to. If any problems or worries arise, it is always best to seek veterinary advice.

BEHAVIOURAL PROBLEMS IN DOGS

Aggression

There are various forms of aggression that may be exhibited by dogs, and some of these are more readily understood than others.

Obviously, the most worrying from the owner's point of view is aggression that is directed towards people, but it is also difficult if you own a dog that is continually fighting with other dogs. On the whole, bitches are less inclined to be aggressive than male dogs and are more ready to accept a subordinate position in the household, but there are wide variations between individual animals. Some dogs are born with a placid disposition while others inherit dominant or assertive characteristics that can lead to aggressive behaviour. Aggression can arise as a result of bad experiences at the hands of thoughtless or unkind people, and a great deal depends on the dog's early upbringing. An owner should always endeavour to correct any form of aggressive behaviour, whether this is growling, barking or snapping, by speaking very severely to the dog and even giving it a smack. The dog should be left in no doubt that its owner strongly disapproves of such outbursts.

Many dogs react in this way to people making deliveries, especially postal workers or other callers in uniform, and this is a form of misplaced territorial aggression. The dog is guarding its home territory, and the behaviour is encouraged and reinforced in the animal's mind because the person soon departs again. Often, if the caller stands his or her ground and does not feel intimidated, the dog backs off in confusion. Indeed, some dogs bark furiously simply because they are themselves afraid and feel threatened. Unfortunately, if, understandably, the person on the receiving end of the dog's behaviour feels frightened, the situation is usually made worse. It is not acceptable or desirable for your dog to cause fear and upset to people calling at your home. If, in spite of your best efforts, your dog continues to rush out furiously barking at the postman or other callers, you should ensure that it is always kept shut away from the front door. (Of course, paradoxically, circumstances arise when this behaviour is useful and a home with a barking dog is far less likely to be burgled.)

If a dog steps over the line of barking and growling and actually bites someone, this is a good deal more serious and the owner becomes involved in a most unpleasant and worrying situation. Unless there are very good mitigating circumstances governing a particular incident, it may be necessary to have the dog painlessly put to sleep. This is certainly the case if you know that your dog cannot be trusted, especially when it is appreciated that the people most commonly bitten and sometimes savaged are young children. This is undoubtedly a hard and painful decision for the owner, who is likely to be fond of the dog, but it is the only correct solution.

A dog that is in great pain or extremely afraid may snap or bite, for instance on a visit to the veterinary surgery. It is best to avoid this possibility if you have reason to suspect that it might arise by placing a muzzle on the dog. A muzzle can be bought in a pet shop but one can also be improvised on the spot using tape, bandage or a strip of strong material (*see below*). Once a muzzle is in place, the owner can have more confidence in handling the dog and trying to calm it down, and the situation is less stressful for all concerned.

Applying a muzzle made from a tape or bandage

Tie a half-hitch in the tape, making sure that the ends are kept quite long.

Firmly restrain the dog, then place the loop of the tape around the dog's nose. Pull the ends to draw the loop tight and close the dog's jaws.

Gently pull the ends downwards and cross them over beneath the lower jaw. Pull the ends backwards, keeping the tape tight.

Tie a tight bow at the back of the dog's head—the knot should be made in front of the dog collar. Check that the muzzle is secure.

Chasing cars and motorbikes

Some dogs develop the habit of chasing after cars or motorbikes and may try to bite the tyres. It is very difficult to eliminate this behaviour once it has become a habit, and so every effort should be made to stop it as soon as it appears. The most effective deterrent is when the dog has an unpleasant experience while indulging in this behaviour. One way to achieve this is to use a 'shock collar.' This is a special collar that is fitted to the neck of the dog and is capable of delivering an electric shock. The shock is triggered from a hand-held control box operated by the owner, by means of radio waves. This device can be very effective when used correctly but should be employed with caution. If it is not possible to use a shock collar or the behaviour has become ingrained, the only solution is to make sure that the dog is never allowed to run free near to traffic.

Chasing sheep *see* DOGS AND OTHER ANIMALS, page 20.

Destructiveness

In older dogs this usually takes the form of chewing furniture, shoes or household items, or wallpaper and the bottom of doors. It should be distinguished from the natural chewing stage that puppies go through during their development, which often occurs around the time of teething. Puppies should not be given access to valued items and should be given toys and chews that they are allowed to bite on. In older dogs, destructive behaviour may arise for a number of reasons, including feelings of insecurity or boredom. Generally it occurs when the owner has gone out and the dog is left alone. The problem may resolve itself. If, for example, the dog is new to its home and is feeling anxious, it may cease to be destructive once it has settled in and knows that it is secure. If the problem persists, it is best to place the dog's bed in a room or porch where it can do the least potential damage and to remove any valued items. The dog should be provided with its own toys and chews that it knows it is allowed to bite on. Leaving the radio on to provide reassurance for the dog may help while the owner is away. At first, the owner should try a series of random short absences that last for only five or ten minutes. The dog should be told to go to its bed when its owner departs but without any petting or fuss being made. When the owner returns and if no bad behaviour has occurred, the dog should be praised and possibly even rewarded with a titbit. The length of absence should gradually be increased as long as no destruction occurs. If the dog has misbehaved, it should be ignored when the owner returns and told to stay in bed. With patience, destructive behaviour can usually be curbed. Also, it is important to try to prevent destructiveness from arising by giving the dog plenty of exercise and an adequate amount of attention each day. A tired and contented dog is much less likely to be destructive.

Excessive barking

It is natural for dogs to bark but if this is excessive it can be extremely irritating to neighbours, especially if it occurs at night. A dog may bark if left alone by its owners for a long period of time. It may be possible to correct this by a series of planned absences (as with destructiveness) and to praise and reward the dog when it does not bark. Of course, if barking is a problem while the owner is present, the dog should be sternly checked and sent to its bed.

Eating inappropriate substances

Some dogs eat their own faeces (a condition called coprophagia), while others eat cow or horse dung or similar inappropriate materials. This behaviour is not likely to cause much harm, although it may be alarming for owners. In some cases, there may be an underlying medical reason for coprophagia and the dog may be attempting to correct a digestive problem. There may, however, be nothing wrong with the dog, and in this case it is better to discourage the practice by removing droppings or covering them with pepper or some other unpleasant substance. If this fails, the dog can be given a drug that makes it feel sick immediately after it has eaten droppings. The dog learns to associate the unpleasant feelings of sickness with eating the faeces, and usually one or two such experiences are sufficient to deter it from this behaviour.

Inappropriate sexual behaviour

Occasionally a male dog may seem to be over-sexed and clasp the leg of a person and show obvious signs of sexual arousal. This is thought to be more likely to occur in a dog that is removed from its mother and brothers and sisters at too young an age and so misses out on an important phase in its development. A young puppy that is reared mainly with people and does not mix with other dogs is more likely to show this misdirected sexual behaviour. Castration lessens or eliminates this behaviour in about two-thirds of dogs, and in the remainder additional hormone treatment (with synthetic progesterones or progestagens) often helps. However, since this is also learned or conditioned to a certain extent, it may be necessary to attempt to eliminate it by behavioural modification training. As soon as the dog shows signs of starting mounting behaviour, it should be banished to a different room on its own for a short period of time. Although such banishment may have to be quite frequent at the start of training, since the dog wishes to be in the company, it usually soon learns that its behaviour is not acceptable.

Straying

As mentioned previously, both male dogs and bitches may show a tendency to stray when driven by the urge to mate. Some males of certain breeds, however, e.g. Labrador retrievers, or particular individuals seem to have an increased tendency to wander. The tendency can be checked by giving the dog plenty of exercise and training, but it may be necessary to ensure that it is let loose only in a secure area. Neutering (*see* page 120) reduces the tendency to wander in the majority of male dogs. Hormone treatment with synthetic progesterones or progestagens is also effective in curbing this behaviour in both bitches and male dogs.

PARASITES

The parasites that affect dogs can be divided into two types. Internal parasites live inside the dog, mainly within the digestive tract, while external ones inhabit the fur and skin.

Internal parasites

The internal parasites that commonly affect dogs are worms belonging to two main groups: roundworms, or ascarids, and tapeworms. These develop into mature worms inside the digestive system of the dog where they live by absorbing partially digested food over their whole body surface. Each has a different and quite complex life cycle that may involve another host animal, and an understanding of this is important in the control of worm infestation. All dogs contract worms at some stage but usually, unless the infestation is very severe, they cause little harm and can be effectively dealt with using modern drugs. These are often in the form of tablets that are mixed with the dog's food but may be given as a liquid or syrup. Worms can be a problem in a dog that is in poor health for some other reason, and young puppies are at particular risk from roundworm infestation (*see below*).

Roundworms

These are a white or greyish colour and usually about 5–15 cm (2–6 ins) in length but may be even larger. They often appear to be looped or coiled and may change to a pink or reddish colour if the worm has recently absorbed food. The species that usually inhabits dogs is called *Toxocara canis*, and worms grow to maturity in the dog's intestine, producing minute eggs that are then passed out with faeces. The eggs have a sticky surface and may adhere to the fur of a dog and be licked up and swallowed. Other dogs are infected when sniffing and nosing around on ground on which eggs have previously been deposited. Eggs can persist for a long time on infected ground and are very resistant to decay, posing a health risk to young children (*see page 69*). Once swallowed by a dog, tiny larvae hatch out from the eggs and are carried around the body in the bloodstream. They migrate through tissues and organs, including the muscles, liver, heart and lungs, from where they are coughed up into the mouth and swallowed once again. In adult dogs, most larvae become lodged in the tissues and form cysts that remain dormant, causing no further harm. Larvae that are coughed from the lungs into the mouth and re-swallowed develop into adult worms in the intestine, and these produce more eggs to repeat the cycle. Mature worms are sometimes vomited by the dog or may be passed intact in faeces. In adult dogs, roundworms generally remain encysted and do not affect the dog in any way. Worms that may be present in the digestive system are safely and effectively eliminated by routine worming with a suitable drug. A veterinary surgeon can advise on the type of preparation to use and on frequency of use.

Particular circumstances apply to a pregnant bitch and to young puppies. Most dogs are infected with roundworms from their mother before and after birth because during pregnancy encysted larvae become active and pass from the tissues into the bloodstream of the bitch. They cross the placenta and pass to the foetuses, lodging in the developing liver and lungs. Shortly before birth, they enter the intestine of the puppy and develop into mature roundworms. Other larvae enter the mammary glands of the mother and are passed to suckling puppies in the milk. Hence two or three weeks after birth, young puppies can have a severe infestation of roundworms and, if left untreated, this can prove fatal.

Symptoms of such infestation include failure to thrive and weight loss, although the puppy has a swollen, pot-bellied appearance, diarrhoea, pain causing crying, loud breathing and coughing. The only way to deal with this infestation is by regular repeated worming of both the bitch and puppies before and after birth. Worming must be repeated periodically to make sure that all the worms that develop in the gut are killed and eliminated. A veterinary surgeon can advise on the most suitable preparations to use for both the bitch and the puppies.

It is necessary to be vigilant about the elimination of roundworms, not only for the sake of the dog but also because of the risk to human health. Those most at risk are young children who may pick up the eggs while playing on contaminated ground and then transfer them to their mouth. Any ground that has been used by dogs should be regarded as suspect since eggs persist long after faeces have decayed. It is evident that puppies are likely to be infected with roundworms, and if young children have access to them then great care must be taken over hygiene. It is especially important to make sure that children wash their hands thoroughly and scrub beneath their fingernails after handling puppies. *Toxocara canis* can complete its life cycle only in dogs. If eggs are swallowed by a child, however, the larvae hatch and travel in the bloodstream in the same way as in the dog, lodging and encysting in various organs of the body. This can cause considerable damage to, e.g. the lungs, liver and retina of the eye where abnormal granulation tissue, called granuloma, may be produced. Symptoms include muscular pain, fever, skin rash, respiratory problems, vomiting and convulsions, depending on the organs affected. Infection can be treated with various drugs, such as diethyl-carbamazine and thiabendazole, but tissue damage may be permanent. It is believed that young children may be at greater risk as their immune system is immature, whereas adults are likely to be more resistant.

Tapeworms

These are long, thin, flat worms that are usually a white colour and resemble lengths of tape. The adult worm consists of a head or scolex, which bears tiny hooks and suckers that attach it to the intestine of the dog. Behind the head there are a series of segments, called proglottids, that each contain male and female reproductive organs. The segments are continually produced from behind the head and mature as they pass backwards. Those at the end farthest away from the head are fully mature and contain fertilized eggs. These segments are shed in the faeces of the dog and usually resemble grains of white rice that may be seen to move and contract. Tapeworms require an intermediate or secondary host in order to complete their life cycle and do not pass directly from one dog (the primary host) to another.

In the case of the most common tapeworm affecting dogs, called *Dipylidium caninum*, the intermediate host is a flea or louse. Other tapeworms, some belonging to the genus Taenia, may have rabbits, birds, mice or sheep as intermediate hosts. If the intermediate host is a mammal, the proglottids dissolve in the stomach or intestine, releasing the eggs. Minute larvae or embryos hatch, which pass through the wall of the digestive tract and enter the blood circulation. They are carried around the body and encyst in muscles and tissues. If this tissue is subsequently eaten by a dog, the tapeworms mature and develop within the intestine. Dogs that hunt and kill rabbits or eat carcasses are commonly infected in this way. In the case of fleas and lice, the minute eggs of the tapeworm are probably consumed during the larval stage when the immature insects are feeding on organic debris on the dog or within its environment. The flea containing the cysts of the tapeworm is swallowed by the dog while it licks and grooms itself. It is uncommon for tapeworms to cause symptoms of ill health or digestive upset in dogs. A number of preparations are available that are specifically designed to eliminate tapeworms, and a veterinary surgeon can advise on which one to use. It can be seen from the above, however, that it is also necessary to deal with the intermediate hosts of the parasite, usually fleas. It may prove difficult to prevent a country-living dog from hunting and eating rabbit, so regular worming is necessary if this is believed to be the source of infection.

Human beings are not usually at risk from the tapeworms that commonly affect dogs. Humans are the primary host of several types of tapeworm, including *Taenia saginata* (the beef tapeworm), *Taenia solium* (the pork tapeworm) and *Diphyllobothrium latum* (the fish tapeworm). In these species, the intermediate hosts are cattle, pigs and fish respectively, and people are infected by eating raw or poorly cooked flesh containing tapeworm cysts. It is important to emphasize, however, that one type of tapeworm species that affects dogs is dangerous to humans, and this is a very small species called *Echinococcus granulosus*. This tapeworm is common in sheep-farming regions of Britain, especially Wales. Sheepdogs are the primary hosts, harbouring the adult worms, which usually consist of only three segments and are less than 5 mm long. Sheep are the normal intermediate hosts, but people can be infected by ingesting the microscopic eggs of the worm, which may be present on the dog's coat or deposited on the ground. In humans, larvae are released from the eggs in the stomach and intestine and make their way through the wall, entering the blood circulation. They lodge in various organs of the body, including the liver, kidneys, lungs and brain, and slowly grow into cysts (called hydatid cysts) that may reach an enormous size and cause considerable disruption. The extent of this damage depends on the site of the cyst, but in the brain it may be very severe, causing blindness, epilepsy or even death. If a hydatid cyst ruptures, it may cause a serious allergic reaction, including skin rashes, fever and respiratory symptoms. Also, there is a further release of numerous larvae, resulting in the growth of more cysts. Treatment is by means of surgery (although some sites may be inoperable) and, once again, children are at greatest risk.

Combined drug preparations are available that effectively eliminate both roundworms and tapeworms in a single dose. These are easy to use—all that is needed usually is to mix one small tablet with the dog's food. These preparations are inexpensive and eliminate worms safely and effectively, along with the anxiety that they can cause, and should form a part of responsible dog ownership.

Other internal parasites

A number of other worm parasites can affect dogs but these tend to be fairly uncommon. They include the whipworm, *Trichuris vulpis*, which most commonly occurs in greyhounds used for racing. Adult worms inhabit a 'pouch' in the bowel, called the caecum, and generally cause few symptoms, although some dogs may suffer from diarrhoea. Eggs are passed out with faeces and new worms develop if these are ingested by another dog.

Two types of hookworm can occur in dogs. *Uncinaria* species cause symptoms of diarrhoea with bleeding and failure to thrive and there may be a loss of weight. *Ancyclostoma* species suck blood and are common in dogs in parts of the USA and Australia. These may be ingested as eggs but hookworm larvae can also burrow through the skin and be carried in the blood circulation to the intestine where they develop into adults. They may cause serious weakness and anaemia. and can also be passed by a bitch to her puppies both before and after birth.

Lungworms, *Filaroides osleri*, live in the lower part of the windpipe (trachea), inhabiting small protrusions that jut out into the central space (lumen). These protrusions partially block the airway and may cause coughing and laboured breathing, especially during exercise. The worms produce eggs that hatch into larvae and are coughed up and may be passed to another dog by licking. An infected nursing bitch usually passes the larval worms to her puppies.

Heartworms, *Dirofilaria immitis*, occur in dogs in some parts of Europe, Australia and the USA. The larval stage of the parasite is transmitted from one dog to another via the bite of mosquitoes. Once in the bloodstream, larvae travel to the heart and the pulmonary artery, which connects with the lungs. They develop into adult worms and cause symptoms including severe cough, respiratory problems, weight loss and possibly even death.

Another internal parasite that can affect dogs is popularly called the tongue worm, *Linguatula serrata*, but in reality it is a large, legless mite. It resembles a flattened tongue and lives in the upper nasal passages of the dog. It can reach a length of 12 cm (4¾ ins) and causes symptoms of sneezing, respiratory problems and discharge from the nose. Eggs are passed out in the discharge and taken up by an intermediate host, which is generally a grazing animal such as a sheep, deer, cow, rabbit, horse, etc. Dogs acquire the infection by eating raw meat containing the larval stage of the parasite.

The kidney worm, *Dioctophyma renala,* is a large nematode worm that may reach a length in excess of 90 cm (1 yard) and be 6 mm thick affecting dogs in some parts of Europe, America and Africa. The worm is contracted if a dog eats raw fish infected with the larval stage of the parasite. It inhabits the right kidney or abdomen, causing extensive tissue damage.

Various other types of parasite, including the bladder worm, *Capillaria plica,* and the tracheal worm, *Capillaria aerophila,* may occasionally occur in dogs. Other varieties not normally seen in the UK can occasionally be brought in by dogs imported from abroad.

External parasites
External parasites live on the skin and among the fur of dogs where they make a living either by biting and sucking blood or by feeding on flakes of debris. Various types can occur, including fleas, lice, mites and ticks.

Fleas
Most dogs are probably affected by fleas at some stage in their life, and recent surveys have confirmed that these parasites are indeed very common. Paradoxically, dogs are far more likely to harbour the cat flea, *Ctenocephalides felis,* than the dog flea, *Ctenocephalides canis,* which is relatively rare. A dog may occasionally pick up fleas from other animals, particularly hedgehogs, rabbits, birds or even humans, but the usual source is cats. Fleas do not complete their life cycle on a dog, but females must obtain a meal of blood before they can reproduce. The female flea frequently drops off the host to lay her eggs in the immediate environment of the dog. Common sites are the dog's bed and bedding but also include chairs,

carpets and the spaces between floorboards. Eggs are smooth and non-sticky and if laid directly on the dog soon drop off into the immediate environment. These then hatch into larvae that feed on minute particles of shed skin or food debris. These then pupate and in the summer and autumn, or in warm, centrally heated surroundings, mature fleas hatch from the pupae. These then require a mammal host to breed in their turn. Flea pupae can exist for many months in this state until environmental conditions are favourable for hatching. In favourable conditions, however, the whole life cycle from egg to adult flea takes only two to three weeks. A female flea may produce as many as 500 eggs in her lifetime.

It is evident that in order to control fleas both the dog and its surroundings must be treated. There are many more fleas in the environment of the dog for every one found on the animal itself. Many insecticidal preparations are available for eliminating fleas, and a veterinary surgeon can advise on which ones to use. Preventative measures include insecticidal tablets that are fed to the dog and solutions that can be applied to the skin. These stop it from being colonized and afford protection from fleas for one month. Daily grooming, especially with a metal comb, helps to remove any fleas that may be present and provides an opportunity to check for them. Fleas can be detected on the dog as very small, shiny brown insects that move rapidly. Sometimes they are congregated at the base of the tail, on the underside of the dog or on the inner thighs. Symptoms include scratching, and the irritation may be so intense that the dog bites itself, developing bare, reddened patches of skin. A few dogs may become sensitized and develop a severe allergic reaction to the saliva of the flea. Usually, an owner is more likely to notice the faeces of fleas, which appear as small, black specks resembling grit caught in the dog's fur and consist of remnants of dried blood. If these are sponged with a moist paper towel or cotton wool, a red-brown stain appears, and so it is easy to differentiate between flea faeces and other dirt. It is best to act immediately once the presence of fleas is suspected by treating the dog, its bed and bedding, carpets and other areas of the home with some of the highly effective products that are readily available. As mentioned earlier, fleas can carry the immature stage of the tapeworm *Dipy-*

lidium caninum, and it may be necessary subsequently to worm a dog that has been bitten.

Lice

These are very small insects, with no wings, that spend their whole life on their host animal. Dogs can be affected by two types of lice, both of which are less common than infestation with fleas. The most common type of dog louse is called *Linognathus setosus*, and it feeds by sucking blood. Another form feeds on flakes of dead skin and other debris within the dog's fur and is a biting louse called *Trichodectes canis*. These lice are sometimes found in greater numbers beneath the tail but common sites for both types include the ears, head, neck and shoulder regions. Long-eared, hairy breeds such as cocker spaniels may be more susceptible. Symptoms of lice include scratching and skin irritation with the appearance of bald patches. A severe infestation with bloodsucking lice can cause anaemia and loss of condition and may be serious, especially in elderly or ill dogs and young puppies. The infestation may be noticed because of the presence of apparent dandruff or scurf. This consists of the eggs and egg cases (nits) of the lice, each of which is firmly stuck to a hair. They can be removed using a fine-toothed comb or by cutting off the affected hairs. If it is suspected that a dog has lice, it should be taken to a veterinary surgeon for examination and diagnosis. A particular regime may need to be followed to eradicate these parasites, using insecticidal shampoos or other preparations. The treatment normally needs to be repeated because it kills only the adult insects and not the eggs. Hence, repeating the treatment at suitable intervals ensures that all lice newly emerged from eggs are killed.

Mites

There are several types of mite that can affect dogs, some of which are just visible to the human eye whereas others can be seen only with the aid of a microscope. Mites are not insects but belong to the class *Arachnida*, which includes the spiders, scorpions and ticks. Ticks and mites are the parasitic members of the group whereas most are free-living.

Ear mites

The ear mite, *Otodectes cyanotis*, affects both dogs and cats. These mites are barely visible to the human eye but can sometimes just be seen as minute grey specks moving over the inner surface of the ear canal. They live on debris composed mainly of dead, shed skin and on the lymph fluid that leaks out when the dog scratches its ear excessively. Symptoms of ear mites are scratching the ear, shaking the head and holding it on one side. The ear may become wet and sticky because of fluid leakage or there may be bleeding. A dog with these symptoms should always be taken to a veterinary surgeon for further investigation, and diagnosis is often made with the aid of an instrument called an auroscope or otoscope. The dog is often found to have a build-up of hard, brown wax in its ears, and when a sample of this is examined under a microscope the mites can be readily identified. If the inflammation is very severe, the dog may need to be sedated or given a general anaesthetic to enable a thorough examination to be carried out.

Treatment is by means of ear drops that contain drugs designed to kill the mites. Some preparations combine these with antibacterial drugs, agents for softening ear wax and local anaesthetics. These combinations help to relieve the symptoms and deal with any secondary bacterial infection that may have gained access through the irritated broken skin. It is often necessary to continue the treatment for some time to make sure that all newly emerging mites are killed. Also, both ears should be treated at the same time even if the symptoms appear to be confined to one, and all dogs and cats in the household should be given simultaneous treatment.

Sarcoptic mange mite

The minute, microscopic mange mite, *Sarcoptes scabei canis*, causes the commonest type of mange in dogs and is a canine form of scabies. This is a very contagious skin disease and is readily spread from one dog to another. It can be a problem in kennels where many dogs are kept in close proximity to one another and tends to be more severe in puppies and younger dogs. The mites live and breed in burrows within the skin and cause a very severe irritation that the dog attempts to relieve by scratching. The infestation usually begins on the ear flaps, in the axillae ('arm pits'), where the upper limbs join the body, and on the inner thighs. It may soon spread, however, and the dog's excessive scratching causes the formation of thickened patches, lesions and scaly, bald patches of skin. If these symptoms are noticed, the dog should be taken to a veterinary surgeon as soon as possible so that diagnosis can be made and treatment started. The condition is likely to spread if not promptly checked, and this can result in scarring of the skin and loss of condition, and is unpleasant and distressing for the dog. Diagnosis is usually made by microscopic examination of skin samples from affected areas in which the mites can be detected. Treatment is by means of various drug preparations and dressings that are applied directly to affected areas (the hair usually needs to be clipped off first). The mites cannot survive for long away from their host so that extensive repeated treatment of the dog's environment and surroundings is not usually necessary. The affected animal should be kept away from other pets, however, and its bed thoroughly washed and disinfected. Bedding should either be discarded and burnt or blankets, etc, may be boiled. All dressings, cotton wool, towels, etc, used on the dog should be similarly treated and the collar and lead must be disinfected. It may be necessary to keep up the treatment and hygienic measures for quite some time to be sure that all the mites have been eliminated.

People handling the dog, especially children, need to exercise particular care. Although scabies in humans is caused by a different (but related) species of mite, the canine form can be transmitted to people. The canine mite does not survive for long on a human host but can cause irritation of the skin or even a marked allergic reaction. The mite can penetrate through clothing so it is wise to avoid close contact with an affected dog, to wear strong gloves and to wash hands after handling the animal. Anyone who develops a skin reaction should seek medical advice.

Demodectic mange or follicular mange (demodecosis)
This is caused by another type of microscopic mite called *Demodex canis*. This mite lives in the deeper layers of the skin, inhabiting the hair follicles, and it is believed that nearly all dogs are affected.

Most are thought to develop resistance so that the mites are not able to spread. In those areas of skin that are affected, however, bare patches may appear and there may be a somewhat musty smell. These patches usually clear up and heal quite quickly although they can also persist for some time. Also, they may suddenly appear in a dog that has not apparently been affected before. It is believed that the normal route of infection is from a nursing bitch to her new puppies rather than between older dogs. If the puppies develop lesions, these are usually on the nose, face and front limbs, but some do not develop signs of infection. The mites are apparently able to remain dormant or relatively inactive only to flare up at some later stage. In most cases, the lesions do not itch greatly but sometimes the dog scratches itself and causes a secondary bacterial infection to occur. There may be a thickening of the skin with a discharge of pus from infected spots and abscesses. This can be very serious and may even have a fatal outcome.

The mites rarely come to the surface and can be difficult to eliminate completely, although modern drugs have made this less of a problem than it was in the past. Diagnosis should be made by a veterinary surgeon, and it is best to start treatment as soon as possible. Demodectic mange is more likely to affect the very short-haired breeds of dog such as boxers, Dobermans and dachshunds, but is by no means confined solely to them.

Cheyletiella mites

These are very small but it is just possible to see them with the naked eye. They can affect any dog, although puppies and short-haired breeds may show more severe symptoms. The mites can cause irritation and itchiness of the skin, although some dogs do not seem to feel discomfort. The most characteristic sign of infestation is the appearance of prolific scurf or dandruff, especially along the back of the dog. This consists of the mites and their eggs, and if it is examined closely it can be seen to be moving. The name 'walking dandruff' is an apt description of this infestation. A dog with these symptoms should be examined by a veterinary surgeon and treatment is similar to that given for sarcoptic mange. People handling the dog should exercise caution, and it is wise to wear gloves and wash hands thoroughly. The mite may cause irritation in people with sensitive skin, and young children are likely to be particularly susceptible.

Harvest mite

The harvest mite, *Trombicula autumnalis*, can affect country-dwelling dogs in the later months of the summer or early autumn. It is the larvae of these mites that are parasitic, and dogs normally pick them up as they go through long grass or other dense vegetation. The larvae attach themselves to areas where the skin is less tough, such as on the ear flaps and between the toes, where they feed and grow. Eventually they drop off and develop into adult mites that feed on rotting vegetation. The harvest mite larvae can be detected as tiny reddish-coloured specks that cause inflammation, irritation and scratching. They can be treated with preparations similar to those that are used against other types of mite.

Ticks

Like mites, ticks are parasitic members of the class *Arachnida*, which includes spiders, and are not insects. Two types of tick can affect dogs—hard-bodied, ixodid species and soft-bodied argasid forms. In Britain it is the hard-bodied types that are important, and the most common is the species found on hedgehogs, *Ixodes hexagonus*. Other species, found in moorland and upland areas, are normally parasitic on sheep but can affect dogs living in country areas. Dogs usually acquire ticks during the warm, summer months after going through thick grass and other dense vegetation. A tick has piercing, biting mouthparts and fastens itself firmly onto the dog's skin, often on the inside of the thighs or abdomen, ears, head or neck. A tick may be very small when it first latches on to the dog but is still easily visible as a small dark-coloured protuberance with short, black, moving legs. The tick feeds on blood and its abdomen swells and may become quite large. The colour may remain dark or become orange or pink.

An attempt can be made to remove the tick, but it is important to do this correctly and to make sure that the whole parasite is removed. A common mistake is to try to pull off the tick, but this

merely separates the abdomen from the rest of the body and leaves
the head and mouth parts firmly embedded in the skin. When this
happens, there is a risk of a painful and septic skin abscess developing. The correct method is to 'anaesthetize' the parasite by applying a pad of cotton wool soaked in surgical spirit, alcohol or insecticidal preparation to try to get the mouthparts to relax. The
body of the tick should be grasped with tweezers, moved from side
to side and then twisted in an anti-clockwise direction. A tick eventually drops off the dog when it is sufficiently engorged with blood
to breed and complete its life cycle. A tick bite is very painful, and
the dog will scratch and bite at the parasite if it is in an accessible
spot. Ticks can attach themselves to any suitable passing mammal,
and this includes both dogs and people.

There has been increasing concern recently about a bacterial infection transmitted by ticks called Lyme disease. The bacteria are
passed on by the bite of an infected tick and cause a potentially serious inflammatory illness in people, early signs of which are a
characteristic red skin rash and 'flu-like symptoms. Not all ticks
carry the bacteria, but it is important to take these parasites seriously and to destroy, by burning, any that are removed from a dog.
People who walk in an area where ticks are known to be present are
advised to wear long trousers tucked into boots and to avoid dense
vegetation. Various drug preparations, such as a solution that is
dropped onto the dog's skin between its shoulder blades, can protect the animal from acquiring ticks. A veterinary surgeon can advise on which to use and frequency of treatment.

Flies and bluebottles

Common blowflies or bluebottles are attracted to rotting, organic
matter but also to wounds and sores on a living animal. If a wound
on a dog is left untreated or not noticed, the flies may lay their eggs
in the sore. These soon hatch into larvae or maggots that feed on
the flesh, a situation commonly called 'fly strike'. It may occasionally be a problem in an elderly or debilitated dog or one that is not
supervised. The animal should be taken to a veterinary surgeon so
that the wound can be cleansed and treated, and the dog is likely to
need antibiotics and other medication, depending on its condition.

A-Z OF ILLNESSES, INJURIES AND VETERINARY PROCEDURES

abdominal pain pain in the abdomen can arise from a number of different causes, varying from mild to severe, and treatment is governed by this. The pain may be a symptom of an illness or digestive upset or the dog may have swallowed a foreign object. A well-wrapped, warm hot-water bottle may provide some relief and comfort, but the dog should be taken at once to the veterinary surgery for examination and diagnosis. X-rays may be needed and possibly surgery to correct the problem. Hence the dog should not be given anything to eat or drink in case general ANAESTHESIA is needed.

abscess a collection of pus at a localized site anywhere in the body. It is usually seen as a painful, hot swelling beneath the skin that enlarges, comes to a head and bursts when ripe. The release of pus and usually some blood from the abscess brings relief from pain. As well as having a painful lump, the dog may seem to be off-colour and be running a temperature. The animal should be seen by a veterinary surgeon, who may advise bathing the swelling with hot water and salts or antiseptic and applying dressings (fomentations) until it bursts. Further bathing is then needed, and the wound must be kept open until all the pus has drained out. It may be necessary to pack the wound with sterile gauze to prevent it from closing over too soon. This is in order to prevent a fresh abscess from forming on or near the site. Usually a course of antibiotics will be prescribed to kill off the bacteria that caused the infection.

Abscesses can form easily as a result of bites from other dogs or animals, ticks or wounds that pick up dirt. Sharp grass seeds trapped between the pads may be responsible for an abscess on the paws. (*See also* ROUTINE CARE OF A DOG, Cleaning teeth, page 39).

acne like people, dogs can be affected by this common skin disorder, which results from bacterial infection of the sebaceous glands and hair follicles. Pus-filled spots form that later burst to leave dry crusty scabs. Acne in dogs often affects the area of the nose and around the eyes. It may be difficult to distinguish acne from some other skin conditions so the dog should be seen by a veterinary surgeon. Treatment is by means of various drugs and creams.

Addison's disease a form of this disorder can occur in dogs, and it is caused by a failure of the cortex of the adrenal glands to produce sufficient quantities of adrenocortical hormones. One adrenal gland is situated above each kidney. Adrenocortical hormones are responsible for regulating the salt/water balance, glucose metabolism and for enabling the body to respond to stress. One sign of this disorder in dogs is an increased thirst as a result of a greater loss of water caused by insufficiency in regulatory mechanisms.

allergic reaction *see* ANAPHYLACTIC SHOCK.

alopecia *see* BALDNESS.

anaemia a decrease in the ability of the blood to carry oxygen because of a reduction in the number of red blood cells or in the amount of haemoglobin that they contain. Haemoglobin is the iron-containing pigment in red blood cells that binds to oxygen. Anaemia is a symptom of some underlying disorder or illness, and three main types are recognized in dogs. The first is the result of actual loss of blood from ruptured blood vessels. This is obvious in the case of an external wound, but bleeding producing anaemia can occur internally following injury (*see* FIRST AID, bleeding, page 141). A great infestation with external or internal bloodsucking parasites can cause this type of anaemia, as can ingestion of certain poisons by a dog, e.g. Warfarin, which is sometimes put down to kill rats and causes haemorrhage and prevents blood from clotting.

The second type of anaemia results from some form of damage or deficiency in the bone marrow, which is responsible for the production of red blood cells. Once again, the cause may be some form of poisoning but others are tumours and dietary deficiencies.

The third type, haemolytic anaemia, occurs if for some reason the dog's immune system destroys its own red blood cells. This can be caused by certain metabolic and inherited disorders and some CANCERS. A similar condition can be caused by certain blood parasites in some countries of the world. Also, toxic substances released by bacterial and some chemical poisons can produce this type of anaemia.

Symptoms of anaemia include pallor of the lips, tongue and gums and also the inner eyelids, tiredness, lack of energy and excess panting. A dog exhibiting these symptoms should be taken to a veterinary surgeon, but treatment depends upon the underlying cause. It is important to make sure that the dog is given a balanced nutritious diet containing plenty of iron.

anaesthesia and anaesthetic anaesthesia is the loss of sensation or feeling in the whole or part of the body, usually as a result of the administration of anaesthetic drugs, so that surgery can be performed. A general anaesthetic produces a loss of sensation in the whole of the body and a local anaesthetic in only one part. General anaesthetics also cause a loss of consciousness, and often combinations of drugs are used to achieve an optimum effect. These depress the activity of the central nervous system, have an analgesic effect, i.e. deaden pain and relax muscles, enabling surgical procedures to be carried out with no awareness on the part of the patient. Local anaesthetic blocks the transmission of nerve impulses in the area where they are applied so that little or no pain is felt.

The great majority of surgical procedures carried out on dogs are performed under general anaesthesia. This removes the fear and trauma that the dog might suffer if it remained conscious and ensures that the animal remains perfectly still. In some cases it may be necessary to administer a general anaesthetic even to examine and investigate a painful disorder, particularly if the dog is aggressive and/or very frightened. As with human patients, a dog should not be given anything to eat or drink for a number of hours before a general anaesthetic to ensure that it has an empty stomach. This reduces the risk of vomiting and of material being inhaled into the lungs, causing pneumonia. Modern drugs used to induce general anaesthesia are normally very safe, and the slight risks attached to their use are greatly outweighed by the benefit of being able to operate to correct painful injuries and disorders in dogs and other animals. Veterinary surgeons are highly skilled and trained in the correct use of these drugs. However, all general anaesthesia poses an element of risk and, as with people, it is usually impossible to identify in advance a dog that may react badly to a particular drug. Elderly dogs, young puppies and those suffering from an existing illness or weakness are likely to be at greater risk. In all cases, a general anaesthetic will not be given unless there is no alternative and it is considered to be in the animal's best interest. Hence, a dog's owner is asked to sign a form consenting to both anaesthesia and surgery, and this gives an opportunity for the details of the procedure to be explained and for any questions to be answered.

The use of local anaesthetic drugs in dogs is generally restricted to the treatment of skin complaints such as the removal of small tumours, etc.

anal gland disorders both dogs and bitches possess a pair of small glands located on either side of and slightly below the anus beneath the tail. These produce a pungent secretion that is released to the outside via a small duct and a minute opening in the skin. The purpose of the glands and the secretion is for scent-marking the territory, and they empty when the dog defecates. In normal circumstances there should be no smell and no visible sign of the presence of the glands. One problem that commonly occurs is that of anal gland congestion. The glands become visibly enlarged and there may be an unpleasant smell. The swelling is irritating for the dog, which tries to relieve its discomfort by dragging its bottom along the ground. Typically, the dog also bites and licks the area or, when walking, stops and turns to look at its tail. The anal glands need to be emptied manually by squeezing gently, and since this can be a recurring problem, an owner may wish to be shown how to do this by a veterinary surgeon. It is important to deal with this problem promptly as there is a tendency for the secretion to harden and infection to occur, causing an ABSCESS to develop. This is acutely painful and hot, and the dog often tries to avoid defecation and may become constipated. This requires immediate veterinary treatment, and the dog will probably need a general ANAESTHETIC so that the abscess can be opened, drained and cleaned.

anal fissure and fistula an anal fissure is a small break or tear in the mucous membrane just within the anus. The dog experiences pain on defecation, and there may be slight bleeding when the motion is passed. The animal should be examined by a veterinary surgeon, and treatment involves the use of ointment or creams, etc, until the crack heals. An anal fistula is an abnormal opening from the rectum through to the surface of the skin in the region of the anus. It may develop after an ABSCESS in this area and requires corrective surgery under general ANAESTHETIC.

anaphylactic shock this is an extreme allergic reaction that may uncommonly occur in a dog following an insect sting, injection or ingestion of drugs or, rarely, some unusual type of food. The animal experiences breathing difficulties, collapse, the gums turn blue and the heartbeat is irregular. The dog fails to respond and is evidently extremely ill. This is an emergency situation, and the dog requires an injection of adrenaline, which must be administered quickly in order to save its life. (*Compare* NETTLERASH.)

anus, imperforate a rare congenital disorder in a puppy in which the anus fails to open during development in the womb. The puppy is unable to pass any waste material from the bowel and there is swelling in the region of the anus. Treatment is by means of a surgical operation under general ANAESTHETIC to create an opening.

appetite loss a loss or lowering of appetite probably occurs in all dogs from time to time and the causes vary. Sometimes the cause may be obvious, for instance, it may be apparent that the dog has a painful mouth and so is reluctant to eat. A dog that has eaten something that disagrees with it and has been sick may refuse its next meal. (If a dog has been sick, it is usually advisable to withhold food for a few hours—*see* VOMITING.) A dog that has been less active than usual may eat less, and a lowering of appetite may occur in very hot weather. Loss of appetite in dogs is, however, often a first sign of illness and may or may not be accompanied by other symptoms such as lethargy, raised body temperature and heartbeat rate, and dull eyes and coat. Sometimes a dog may appear to behave normally but still refuses food. As a rule, it is better to observe the dog closely, note symptoms and take the animal to a veterinary surgeon so that the problem can be diagnosed and treated.

It should also be appreciated that a dog can lose its appetite as a result of psychological or emotional trauma, e.g. being placed in kennels or separated from its owner. Usually this is only a passing problem that can be overcome by sympathetic handling by those caring for the dog. (*See also* DIET, page 28)

arthritis this is inflammation of the joints and is a relatively common condition in elderly dogs. There are various forms and causes of arthritis, including injury or trauma and infection. Symptoms are pain, swelling, heat and restricted movement in the affected joint, and the dog may be quite lame. Osteoarthritis involves the joint cartilage, with accompanying changes in the associated bone. There is a loss of cartilage, and the function of the joint becomes impaired and painful. Rheumatoid arthritis is another form, involving the synovial membrane, cartilage and bone around a joint, which shows a typical pattern of changes. Both forms are similar in human beings and dogs. There is no cure for arthritis, which tends to flare up periodically in acute phases. A veterinary surgeon will advise on the best course of treatment, and various drug preparations are available to relieve the symptoms.

asphyxia a state of suffocation during which breathing eventually stops and oxygen fails to reach the tissues and organs. Causes include drowning, strangulation (which can occur with an incorrectly used choke chain), an inhaled object blocking the windpipe and breathing in poisonous fumes. It can also occur as a result of ANAPHYLACTIC SHOCK, when the throat may swell and prevent air passing through the windpipe to the lungs. It is an emergency condition requiring prompt intervention by artificial respiration to save the dog's life (*see* FIRST AID, page 140).

asthma this condition is uncommon in dogs but may occur as a result of an allergic reaction. There is laboured and difficult breathing and the dog is in obvious distress. A veterinary surgeon should always be consulted if a dog develops problems in breathing.

Aujesky's disease *see* PSEUDO-RABIES.

babesiosis a fever transmitted by ticks (*see* PARASITES, page 77) that occurs in Asian, Latin American and southern European countries. It causes symptoms of jaundice, anaemia and a rise in temperature, and the dog is lethargic and ill.

bad breath it is not uncommon for dogs to develop bad breath, and this is nearly always related to disorders of the teeth and gums. A veterinary surgeon should be consulted so that any problems can be treated, and various preparations are available that can help to alleviate the odour. Brushing the teeth with toothpaste formulated for dogs can help to control bad breath.

balanitis inflammation and infection of the sheath of the penis, which is fairly common in young male dogs. Symptoms are a thick discharge from the penis that is white in colour and contains pus, and the dog frequently licks and cleans himself in this area. The dog should be seen by a veterinary surgeon, and the condition can be cleared up with antibiotic treatment.

baldness elderly dogs can occasionally suffer from a loss of hair or baldness. Usually, however, the appearance of bald patches or alopecia in the dog is the result of some form of skin disorder often caused by external parasites (*see* page 71). A less common cause is hypothyroidism (myxoedema) in which there is a lack of the hormones produced by the thyroid gland.

bee and wasp stings dogs may be at risk from stings because of the tendency to chase after and snap and bite at insects. Stings on the body are painful but, unless they are numerous, should not usually prove harmful. A bee sting is likely to be left in the skin and should be removed with tweezers, taking care not to squeeze the poison sac. Stings can be bathed with cold water or a solution of half a pint of water containing one teaspoonful of sodium bicarbonate. The danger arises if the dog is stung on its tongue as this may then swell and block the windpipe, causing breathing difficulties. A further risk is that of ANAPHYLACTIC SHOCK, which can be caused by an insect sting. A dog with breathing difficulties needs immediate veterinary attention. It may be necessary to attempt artificial respiration in order to save its life (*see* FIRST AID, page 140). Unfortunately, however, if there is a great deal of swelling in the region of the throat, this may not be successful.

biopsy an aid to diagnosis that involves removing a small sample of living tissue from the body for examination under a microscope. The technique can be used to distinguish between benign and malignant TUMOURS. In dogs, this procedure would normally be carried out under a general ANAESTHETIC. (*See also* DIAGNOSTIC TESTS.)

bites most dogs are likely to get bitten at some time in their life, either during a fight with another dog or by some other animal. Superficial bites should be bathed with an antiseptic solution, but deeper or more extensive wounds may require veterinary attention and stitching. The main risk from a bite is the likelihood of subsequent bacterial infection and the development of an ABSCESS. An infected bite will become hot and increasingly painful, with a discharge of pus. In this situation the dog should be treated by a veterinary surgeon, as a course of antibiotics is needed to combat the infection, and the wound will require thorough cleaning and dressing. Rarely, in upland and moorland countryside, a dog may be bitten by an adder. If this occurs, the animal should be kept calm and quiet and taken to a veterinary surgeon immediately. The dog will usually require an injection of an antidote for adder venom.

bladder stones as in humans, bladder stones or calculi composed of deposits of mineral salts can form anywhere in a dog's urinary tract and cause a partial or total blockage. The symptoms are straining but passing only small quantities of urine that may be tinged with blood. The dog may be unable to urinate at all, and the bladder may then become distended and there is discomfort and pain. These symptoms resemble those of CYSTITIS in the first instance but the condition is more severe. The dog needs immediate veterinary attention and may require an operation under a general ANAESTHETIC to remove the stones. In susceptible dogs, bladder stones can be a recurring problem, although special diets can help.

bleeding *see* FIRST AID, page 141.

blepharitis an infection and inflammation of the eyelids in which there is a sticky discharge that may glue them together. The dog should be examined by a veterinary surgeon, and an antibiotic ointment is normally prescribed to clear up the infection. (For bathing eyes and applying ointment, *see* page 40).

blindness this can arise from a variety of different causes, including injury, diseases such as DISTEMPER that do not directly involve the eyes, and ageing (*see* CATARACT). Dogs are probably better equipped to deal with blindness than people, having acute senses of smell and sound detection. Hence it may be possible for a blind dog to have a reasonably good quality of life depending upon individual circumstances.

blisters these small, fluid-filled sores beneath the surface of the skin do not usually occur in dogs but may arise as a result of a burn or frictional injury. A minor blister can be bathed with warm water containing an antiseptic solution, dried and covered with a clean dressing. (*See* FIRST AID, burns and scalds, page 145).

blood samples and transfusions in the case of illness, it may sometimes be necessary to obtain blood samples to aid diagnosis or to check on a dog's progress, and this is carried out by a veterinary surgeon. Similarly, a dog that is very ill may occasionally require blood transfusions, generally as a result of serious injuries or during or after a major operation.

breathing problems these are a fairly common occurrence in dogs, and the cause should always be investigated. Symptoms include laboured, noisy breathing, especially after exercise, and coughing and panting. Some of the causes are infections such as DISTEMPER and bronchitis, infestation by a variety of internal parasites (*see* page 65) and heart disease.

brucellosis, canine a form of brucellosis in dogs that is caused by the bacterium *Brucella canis*. It is a sexually transmitted disease that causes infertility and also spontaneous abortion in pregnant bitches. Even if a pregnancy is sustained to term, puppies are usually stillborn or do not survive for very long. The discharge produced by a bitch following birth contains numerous bacteria, and other dogs may be directly infected through contact with this. Rarely, these bacteria can produce mild symptoms of infection in people, including fever and swollen glands. However, this is not the usual form of the disease that can be contracted from sheep and cattle. Canine brucellosis is uncommon in Britain but occurs quite frequently elsewhere, e.g. in the USA.

burns and scalds *see* FIRST AID, page 145.

bursitis inflammation of a bursa, which is a hollow in the fibrous tissue surrounding a joint and has a smooth lining that reduces friction. Bursitis may occur at the knee and elbow, particularly in a dog that lies down a great deal, and puts pressure on these areas. The region becomes stiff and swollen with a collection of fluid within the joint. Veterinary attention is needed, and pads and bandages help to relieve the pressure on the affected part. An equivalent condition in humans is housemaid's knee.

Caesarean delivery a procedure that is normally carried out as an emergency by a veterinary surgeon when it is apparent that labour and birth are not going to proceed successfully. This may be because of an awkward presentation, so that a puppy has become stuck, or ineffective contractions of the womb (uterine inertia). The bitch is given an ANAESTHETIC, and the puppies are delivered via an incision through the wall of the abdomen and another made directly into the womb. The wounds are sutured, and the bitch and puppies require extra care.

cancer a widely used term describing any form of malignant TU-MOUR. Characteristically, there is an uncontrolled and abnormal growth of cancer cells that invade surrounding tissues and destroy them. Cancer cells may spread throughout the body via the bloodstream or lymphatic system, a process known as metastasis, and set up secondary growths elsewhere. As with human beings, dogs are subject to a range of cancerous conditions. The most common are cancer of the mammary glands (in bitches), bones and bone marrow, lymph nodes, digestive organs, mouth, gums and throat, skin and testicles in males. As in human medicine, treatment takes the form of surgery, radiotherapy and chemotherapy. If caught early, some malignancies can be successfully treated by surgical removal, and this applies to tumours of the mammary glands and skin. Usually the outlook is not optimistic for internal forms of cancer, and treatment is aimed at relieving symptoms and prolonging life. This is only worthwhile, however, if the dog can enjoy a reasonable quality of life after treatment. Although more advanced therapies are becoming increasingly available, in many instances it is kinder to have a dog painlessly put to sleep.

In general, cancer is more likely to affect middle-aged and elderly dogs, but there is considerable variation in this, and some breeds appear to be more susceptible to particular types of tumour. Growths affecting the mammary glands and reproductive organs are often hormone-dependent. Spaying reduces the incidence of mammary tumours in bitches, particularly if this is performed before the animal comes into heat for the first time.

canine adenovirus (CAV-1, CAV-2) the virus responsible for IN-FECTIOUS CANINE HEPATITIS, and, if inhaled, one of the organisms that can cause KENNEL COUGH in dogs. These diseases can be prevented by vaccination, and regular booster doses ensure that a dog receives the best possible protection. Even so, it is believed that many non-vaccinated dogs are infected with these viruses but develop a natural immunity and exhibit few or no symptoms. However, some dogs are likely to become severely ill, and young animals less than twelve months old are at greatest risk.

canine respiratory disease (CRD) *see* KENNEL COUGH.

canker a popular term for a range of ear problems in dogs, particularly those in which there is a sticky and possibly smelly discharge. *See* EXTERNAL PARASITES—Ear mites, page 74.

car sickness some dogs are particularly prone to car sickness, and this can be quite a difficult problem to overcome. The dog should not be fed before the journey so that it travels on an empty stomach. Also, various drug preparations are available that can help, and a veterinary surgeon can advise on which of these to use. It is probably best to avoid car journeys if a dog is persistently and frequently sick.

castration *see* NEUTERING.

cataract a condition in which the lens of the eye becomes opaque or clouded, resulting in a blurring of vision. It may arise from a number of different causes, including injury, congenital, i.e. hereditary, factors, diseases such as diabetes, and conditions affecting the nutrition of the eye. The most common cause, however, in dogs as in people, is the advancement of age, during which changes take place naturally in the lens, involving the protein components. The changes may be noticed as a spot or greenish-bluish discoloration, but usually the dog can still see. BLINDNESS in the affected eye occurs if the whole of the lens is involved and it will appear to be an off-white colour.

catarrh irritation and inflammation of mucous membranes (but generally taken to refer to the nasal passages and airways) with the production and discharge of a thick mucus. As in people, a discharge from the nose in a dog, often accompanied by sneezing, is an indication of some disorder. There may be other signs of illness, and the condition can be the result of a number of different causes. These include viral infection, DISTEMPER, a foreign body that has become lodged inside the nose or a nasal TUMOUR. A dog with these symptoms should be examined and the condition diagnosed by a veterinary surgeon, with treatment depending on the cause.

choking *see* FIRST AID, page 147.

chorea a disorder of the nervous system characterized by the involuntary, jerky movement of muscles so that the affected part twitches uncontrollably. In dogs, this condition arises as a symptom of DISTEMPER and usually occurs some time after the infection is diagnosed, when the animal appears to be recovering. Sometimes chorea is the only indication that the dog has been infected with distemper. Chorea is one of the milder manifestations of nervous system disorder caused by distemper and, depending on the muscles affected, the dog may still be able to enjoy a reasonable quality of life.

claws *see* ROUTINE CARE OF A DOG—Paws and claws, page 38.

colitis inflammation of the colon, which is the main part of the large intestine where water is re-absorbed from food residues before the waste is passed as faeces. Symptoms include frequent DIARRHOEA, straining and the passage of clear, bloodstained mucus. A dog with symptoms of colitis should be examined and treated by a veterinary surgeon. Various drugs and a special low roughage diet may be used to alleviate the condition.

coma a state of deep unconsciousness from which the dog cannot be roused. It may be accompanied by deep, noisy breathing and strong heart action, and there is a lack of response to painful stimuli and lack of eye reflexes. It can arise from a number of different causes, including injury to the brain, high fever as a result of infection, ingestion of drugs or poisons, or inhalations of fumes such as carbon monoxide, shock and extreme heat or cold. Another common cause is diabetes, and this can be a difficult condition to treat in dogs. A dog in a coma requires immediate veterinary attention for treatment of the cause of the condition. Treatment and outlook vary according to cause, and coma may occur as a result of an emergency requiring artificial respiration and heart massage (*see* FIRST AID, artificial respiration, page 140).

conjunctivitis inflammation of the mucous membrane (conjunctiva) that lines the inside of the eyelid and covers the front of the eye. It is usually the result of an infection that may gain access through an abrasion caused by a foreign body in the eye. The eye can be bathed gently using clean cotton wool and cool boiled water, wiping from the inside to the outside. The dog should be examined by a veterinary surgeon and is likely to need antibiotic eye ointment to kill the infection.

constipation a condition in which the bowels are opened too infrequently and the faeces become hard, dry and difficult and painful to pass. In dogs, the condition is sometimes caused by a blockage of indigestible material such as a piece of bone, matted grass, string, hair, nylon fibre or other material that the dog has swallowed. A TUMOUR, enlarged PROSTATE GLAND (in males) or HERNIA are possible further causes. There may be pain and straining, and small amounts of blood may be passed. The dog should be taken to a veterinary surgeon to ascertain the cause of the problem, and laxatives or other treatment may be needed. A bitch may become constipated in the last days of pregnancy, and older dogs are also more prone to this problem. It is important that an elderly dog is given a good diet containing plenty of roughage and an adequate amount of exercise. It may be possible to treat an occasional bout of constipation with liquid paraffin mixed with the feed, but this should be given only for short periods following veterinary advice.

Occasionally, the opening of the anus may become blocked with faeces and other material stuck to the hair. It is best to sit the dog in warm water and to use a mild shampoo to loosen and dislodge the matted material. The hair can then be trimmed away and lubricating K-Y jelly applied to the area.

convulsions or **fits** these are involuntary, rapid and alternate contractions and relaxations of muscles, throwing the body and limbs into contortions. Usually there is an initial trembling followed by marked contractions of the muscles, generally resulting in the animal collapsing onto the ground and thrashing its limbs and biting its jaws. Sphincter muscles controlling the bladder and anus may relax, causing urine and faeces to be voided, and the dog may salivate. If the dog is on a hard surface or close to jutting-out objects, these should be covered with cushions, blankets or coats to prevent injury. It is best not to interfere with the dog or try to restrain it in any way unless it is in a dangerous position. If this is the case, the dog should have a coat or blanket placed around it and pulled clear of the hazard with this to lessen the chances of the helper being bitten. A fit normally lasts from one to four minutes, and as the muscular activity subsides the dog often appears dazed and may not be able to see properly. It should be kept calm and quiet in a cool darkened room, and the owner should stay with the dog and speak to it reassuringly. At the same time, veterinary advice and assistance should be sought. Occasionally, the fits continue and the condition is then known as *status epilepticus*. This is an emergency, and the animal requires immediate veterinary treatment.

Convulsions occasionally occur in quite young puppies, and in some cases the cause is believed to be roundworm infestation. Usually the fits are not too serious but veterinary attention is needed.

There are many causes of convulsions, including metabolic disorders such as low levels of blood sugar, infectious diseases such as DISTEMPER, which may result in ENCEPHALITIS or MENINGITIS, TETANUS, injury to the brain and disorders of the liver and kidneys. A serious condition, called ECLAMPSIA, that can affect a bitch nursing puppies, also produces convulsions. In many instances it may not be possible to determine the cause of a fit, and treatment depends on the nature of the dog's condition, i.e. whether there is any underlying disease present. Drugs can be given to control recurrent convulsions but may not be necessary if the condition is mild or fits occur infrequently.

coughing as with people, a dog may cough for a number of different reasons, some of which are minor and others potentially more serious. Coughs can occur as a result of inhalation of dust, pollen or other irritating substances, respiratory infections such as a cold or KENNEL COUGH, infestation by certain parasites (*see* page 65) and serious diseases and disorders including DISTEMPER, collapsed trachea (windpipe) and heart problems. If the cough does not occur frequently and is not troubling the dog or is not accompanied by other symptoms of illness, it is acceptable to wait a little while before taking any action as it may subside and disappear. If there are other symptoms, however, and the dog appears unwell and its condition is causing concern, then veterinary attention is needed. Treatment depends on cause but proprietary cough medicines are available for dogs and a veterinary surgeon will advise on which to use. A dog with a cough should not be allowed to rush about and needs to be kept warm and protected from damp and cold.

cryosurgery the use of extreme cold to perform surgical procedures, usually on localized areas to remove unwanted tissue. In dogs, cryosurgery is generally used to remove superficial or readily accessible growths such as those on the skin.

cryptorchidism and monorchidism *see* SEXUAL BEHAVIOUR AND BREEDING—Male dog, page 44.

Cushing's syndrome a metabolic disorder that results from excessive amounts of corticosteroid hormones being released from the cortex of the adrenal glands. The release of these hormones is controlled by the pituitary gland at the base of the brain. The pituitary gland produces a chemical messenger called adrenocorticotrophic hormone, or ACTH, which travels in the bloodstream to the adrenal glands that are situated one above each kidney. When this regulatory mechanism breaks down, Cushing's syndrome may result. One symptom of this in dogs is excessive drinking. It requires treatment by a veterinary surgeon to try to regulate the imbalance.

cyst a small, usually benign, swelling or tumour containing fluid or a soft secretion within a membraneous sac. Several varieties of cyst can occur in dogs, some of which are more troublesome than others:

1 sebaceous cysts are swellings on the skin that may be about the size of a large marble. Some breeds seem to be particularly prone to develop these, e.g. Pekinese, and they can cause discomfort depending on their situation. A veterinary surgeon should be consulted and surgical removal may be necessary.

2 interdigital cysts are quite common in dogs with deep recesses between the toes. These allow foreign bodies such as grit, thorns or seeds to collect, which may nick the skin, allowing access to bacterial infection. The resultant cyst can be quite painful and may make the dog lame as there is a tendency for an ABSCESS to form. A veterinary surgeon should be consulted as to the best course of treatment, which may include soaking the foot in an antiseptic solution, a course of antibiotics or surgical removal. Preventative measures include clipping the hair between the toes of a susceptible dog and frequent inspection and washing of the paws to stop the accumulation of debris.

3 salivary cysts are swellings within the mouth caused by a blockage in a duct leading from a salivary gland. A salivary cyst that forms beneath the tongue is called a ranula. The dog should be

seen by a veterinary surgeon and surgical removal of the cyst may be needed.

4 ovarian cysts sometimes occur on the ovary of a bitch and are one cause of infertility. The bitch may have a disrupted pattern of coming into heat and eventually show other signs of illness. Veterinary treatment is needed, which may involve giving hormones or surgery.

cystitis inflammation of the bladder, normally caused by bacterial infection and more common in bitches than in male dogs. This is because the urethra is much shorter in bitches, allowing easier access for infection. The symptoms of cystitis are frequent attempts to urinate but with only small quantities of urine being passed. The urine may contain blood and have a strong smell, and the process is evidently painful. The dog should be encouraged to drink plenty of water, as this helps to flush out the bacteria, but also needs veterinary attention and a course of antibiotics to kill the infection.

deafness some breeds, particularly those that are white, are prone to a congenital, inherited form of incurable deafness. These include bull terriers and Dalmatians, and the defective gene appears to be linked with the one responsible for coat colour. More usually, however, deafness is a condition of old age in dogs and is linked to degenerative changes in the organs of the inner ear responsible for hearing. A deaf dog can still enjoy a good quality of life, but extra vigilance is needed when the animal is being exercised, particularly with regard to traffic.

dehydration a healthy dog drinks in order to make up water that has been lost from the body through urination, panting and elimination of waste. If a dog is unable to make up this deficit, it will soon begin to show signs of dehydration. A dog that is dehydrated shows a loss of skin elasticity so that if a small portion is pinched, it stays in that position. It will usually have a dry nose and mouth, as fewer secretions are being produced, and the eyes may appear sunken. The dog is likely to be lethargic and generally unwell. Dehydration can result from a number of different illnesses or simply from being denied access to water, especially in hot weather. Vomiting and diarrhoea are common causes of dehydration, but water must be given cautiously if a dog is being continually sick. A dog suffering from dehydration needs to be examined by a veterinary surgeon to determine the cause and treatment. Serious cases may need to be hospitalized and given fluids intravenously.

dew claws these are vestigial thumbs that are situated on the back of the legs five or six centimetres above the paws (*see* ROUTINE CARE OF A DOG—Paws and claws, page 38).

diabetes the two forms of diabetes that occur in people can also affect dogs, and the disease runs a very similar course. Diabetes insipidus is a rare condition that is characterized by an excessive thirst and the passing of copious amounts of urine that does not contain sugar. There is gradual weawxkness and loss of weight. The condition is caused by a deficiency in antidiuretic hormone (vasopressin) produced by the pituitary gland, and the dog should be examined and treated by a veterinary surgeon. Diabetes mellitus is a complex disorder that can affect middle-aged and elderly dogs and is the result of a failure in the mechanism of sugar metabolism. It results in an accumulation of sugar in the blood and urine and is caused by a lack of the hormone insulin, which is secreted by cells in the pancreas. Hence sugars are not available to be broken down to provide energy, and fats are utilized instead. Symptoms include an excessive thirst and passing copious quantities of urine, which, when analysed, is found to contain sugar. The dog has a great appetite but loses weight gradually. Eventually, if the condition remains untreated, the dog will become obviously ill. There is VOMITING, DEHYDRATION, lethargy and a typical 'pear drops' smell on the breath and from urine because of the presence of substances called ketones. The dog passes into a diabetic COMA as a result of the metabolic crisis brought about by excessively high levels of blood sugar. This is an emergency, and the dog requires immediate veterinary treatment in order to save its life.

Diabetes in dogs corresponds to the more severe human form called juvenile-onset diabetes. The only treatment is daily injections of insulin and close monitoring of the animal, including testing the urine for the presence of sugar. This obviously requires considerable commitment from the owner and, depending on individual circumstances, it may be kinder to have the dog put to sleep. In treating a diabetic dog, one problem that can occasionally arise is giving an accidental overdose of insulin. The symptoms of this are disorientation, staggering and confused behaviour, CONVULSIONS and coma leading to death, caused by a sudden reduction in blood sugar. This is also an emergency, the immediate remedy for which is to give the dog sugar in the form of honey, syrup or prepared glucose solution that should be kept readily to hand. In addition, veterinary advice should be sought in case the dog needs further treatment. If any of the symptoms of diabetes are noticed or suspected, there should be no delay in seeking veterinary attention and treatment for the dog. While any dog can develop diabetes mellitus, it most commonly occurs in bitches. About six out of every one thousand dogs develop this condition in a ratio of three bitches to each male.

diagnostic test as in human medicine, a veterinary surgeon may occasionally think it advisable to carry out certain investigative procedures on a dog in order to reach a precise diagnosis of a particular problem. Depending on the nature of the symptoms, a variety of tests could be carried out. These include analysis of samples of blood, urine or faeces, swabs of discharges that may be cultured for bacterial analysis, ultrasound tests and exploratory surgery, particularly to carry out a biopsy of suspect tissue such as a TUMOUR. More complicated tests may sometimes be helpful but no procedures are carried out without full consultation with, and the consent of, the dog's owner. Any investigation that might cause pain or distress is normally carried out under general ANAESTHETIC.

diarrhoea increased frequency and looseness of bowel movements involving the passage of unusually soft or watery faeces. In dogs, as in humans, diarrhoea can have a number of different causes, ranging from a dietary upset (eating an unsuitable, unusual or irritating substance), bacterial food poisoning, disorder of the digestive system, such as COLITIS, and disease, e.g. DISTEMPER or CANCER. If the diarrhoea is not accompanied by other symptoms such as vomiting and the dog does not appear to be ill, treatment can be given at home. No food should be given for twenty-four hours but frequent small drinks of water, perhaps with one teaspoonful of sugar or glucose added, must be offered so that the dog does not become dehydrated. If the diarrhoea lessens, a small quantity of light food should be offered, such as a little steamed fish or chicken with some rice. If this does not provoke a resumption of the symptoms, the dog can gradually be returned to its normal diet. If diarrhoea persists or resumes following this treatment, the dog should be seen by a veterinary surgeon. If there are other accompanying symptoms such as obvious pain or discomfort, passage of blood or if the diarrhoea is explosive, home treatment should not be attempted as the dog needs veterinary treatment.

dislocation a dislocation is the displacement of one of the two bones that form a joint from its normal position. Common sites are the hip, lower jaw, knee (stifle joint) and toe in greyhounds. A dislocation usually occurs as a result of an accidental blow where considerable force has been applied, such as can result from a fall or being struck by a car. Some breeds, however, may be more inclined to suffer a particular form of dislocation than others. Dislocation of the hip joint is more common in young dogs of some larger breeds. Toe dislocation is common in greyhounds, and that of the stifle joint involving the knee cap or patella in toy and small breeds such as miniature poodles. If the hip is dislocated, one leg appears to be shorter than the other, and if the lower jaw is involved, the dog is unable to close its mouth. In the case of the knee joint, the patella moves from its normal position at the front of the leg to the inside, and this can occur when the dog suddenly changes direction when running fast. The characteristic symptoms of dislocation are pain and swelling around the affected joint so that the animal is not able to function normally.

In many instances, especially following an accident, it may be impossible to tell whether a FRACTURE or dislocation has occurred. A dislocation prevents movement at the joint but there are no broken bones and, in general, no bleeding. If a dislocation is suspected, the dog should be made to lie down in its bed or other suitable place and kept as quiet and still as possible. A veterinary surgeon should be called immediately and the dog should not be given anything to eat or drink. A general ANAESTHETIC is usually needed so that the joint can be restored to its normal position without causing further pain. Manipulation of bones is a skilful procedure that should be carried out only by a trained person. Clumsy handling of a dislocated joint may cause further damage. (*See* FIRST AID—broken bones, page 144.)

distemper a highly infectious disease of dogs, wolves, foxes and some other wild animals, e.g. badgers, that is caused by a virus. It is a serious and often fatal disease and a dog is infected by sniffing contaminated discharges from an animal that has distemper. The virus is present in the urine, saliva and nasal mucus of an infected dog and remains active and contagious on the ground and in the general environment. Hence there does not need to be direct contact between animals for the disease to be passed on. The vast majority of dogs that contract distemper (90%) and show identifiable symptoms of the illness are young animals aged less than two years. It is believed that about half of all the dogs exposed to distemper develop antibodies to the virus. The infection is effectively fought off by the dog's immune system without the development of symptoms, or these may be so slight as to pass unnoticed or not diagnosed. Older dogs are less likely to develop distemper because almost all have either been vaccinated or have developed a natural immunity after encountering this very prevalent virus in early life. However, an older dog with a compromised immunity or one that has lived an isolated life where it has not encountered the virus may occasionally develop distemper.

It is known that young puppies carry some antibodies to the disease for the first three months of life but after this are very vulnerable to infection. Effective vaccination is available, however, and the course is usually started at twelve weeks of age. While the virus is always present, distemper tends to flare up in outbreaks, some of which are more virulent than others. Early symptoms in dogs that are infected are quite variable and are more severe in some animals than in others. Hence the diagnosis can be problematic in the early stages, but the illness may be suspected in a dog with an unknown or suspect record of vaccination.

Symptoms usually start about two weeks after the dog has inhaled infected droplets containing the virus. Often the eyes become reddened and there is a discharge both from them and from the nose. This is quite thin and runny at first but later it becomes yellow and thick and contains pus. The dog often develops a COUGH and sneezing and a raised temperature that may rise and subside. There is often APPETITE LOSS and DIARRHOEA, discoloration of the teeth and BAD BREATH. There may also be VOMITING and WEIGHT LOSS. The respiratory symptoms may lead to a secondary bacterial PNEUMONIA, which in itself can prove fatal.

About half of all dogs with distemper eventually develop disorders of the nervous system, especially CHOREA, CONVULSIONS and PARALYSIS. This is a particularly distressing feature of distemper as these disorders often develop some time after the initial infection, when other symptoms have subsided and the dog seems to be recovering. The usual time interval ranges from a few weeks to several months, and the delay in the onset of symptoms is because of the fact that the virus is able to persist in the nervous system where it is less easily removed by the antibodies that have been developed against it. Once again, the severity of the symptoms varies considerably but they often become so severe that the only humane option is to have the dog put to sleep.

In a few cases it may be years before nervous system disorders develop, and these may be the only indication that the dog has been previously infected with distemper. This is sometimes called 'old dog distemper', although in fact affected animals are middle-aged rather than elderly.

In about a quarter of dogs with distemper, a further symptom that develops is a hardening and thickening of the skin on the pads of the paws, a condition known as hardpad. This was once thought to be a separate disease but is now recognized as a manifestation of distemper. The hardening and thickening of the skin is heard as a distinctive tapping noise when the dog walks on hard ground, and in some cases cracks may open up that are painful and cause LAMENESS. Hardening and cracking of the nose may also occur.

ear inflammation (otitis externa) it is quite common for dogs to suffer from inflammation and irritation of the ears, and this can have a variety of causes. These include ear mites (*see* PARASITES—Ear mites page 74), accumulation of wax, injury, especially as a result of a fight, and the presence of a foreign body such as a piece of stick, seed or other vegetation. Any one of these can provide a focus for a subsequent bacterial infection that further exacerbates the condition. Ear discomfort is usually quite easy to detect. The dog usually shakes its head repeatedly or holds it on one side and paws at the affected ear or rubs it against furniture, etc. The ear may be obviously hot and inflamed, and there may be a smelly discharge indicating the presence of an infection. Dog breeds with pendulous ears such as spaniels seem to be more prone to problems, and this is thought to be due to restricted circulation of air. In particular, wax tends to build up and accumulate as the structure of the ear impedes its natural removal. Some other dogs, such as miniature poodles, have a very narrow ear canal while others, including dachshunds and German shepherds, produce copious quantities of ear wax. Hence problems caused by ear wax are relatively common in these breeds, and individual dogs may also be particularly susceptible. Ear inflammation in dogs requires examination by a veterinary surgeon so that the nature of the problem can be diagnosed and the best course of treatment followed. If the condition is very painful, the dog may need to be tranquillized or given a general ANAESTHETIC so that a thorough examination can be carried out. The dog should receive prompt veterinary attention, because if ear inflammation is neglected there is a risk of more serious damage occurring. The condition can become entrenched and chronic, leading to ulceration, scarring and thickening of the lining of the external ear canal. Or the delicate ear drum, which is a thin membrane at the base of the outer ear canal that transmits sound vibrations to the organs of hearing, may rupture. This allows access for infection into the deeper parts of the ear, which can lead to disruption of the organs of balance and, rarely, to DEAFNESS. Treatment of ear inflammation often requires the application of medication in the form of ear drops, which may contain ceruminolytic agents to soften wax, antimicrobial or anti-parasitic drugs and analgesics to lessen pain.

eclampsia ('milk fever') this serious condition can occasionally arise in a bitch shortly after giving birth or, rarely, in late pregnancy. It is caused by a blood deficiency in calcium, a great deal of which is used in forming the skeletal structure of the puppies and in milk production. Eclampsia is most common in small bitches that have produced a large litter and is rare in all large breeds with the exception of the German pointer. The most common time for it to appear is two to four weeks after birth, but it may occur earlier or later. Symptoms may arise suddenly and include restless behaviour and a refusal to settle with the puppies, or the bitch may be sleepy. She may show other symptoms of distress and then develop a lack of coordination and muscular spasms. Eventually, a high temperature and convulsions result, which may rapidly prove fatal. A bitch showing any signs of illness following birth needs immediate veterinary attention. The condition can be successfully treated by giving an injection of calcium but cannot be prevented from developing. Calcium supplements should only be given following veterinary advice, and it is better to make sure that the bitch receives plenty of nourishing food during pregnancy and lactation. Eclampsia may be more likely to occur in a bitch that has not received adequate nourishment but this is not exclusively the case. (*See* PREGNANCY—When to intervene or call a vet, page 56.)

ectropion *see* ENTROPION.

eczema inflamed and irritated skin that is itchy and may 'weep' and does not have an obvious cause, such as the presence of external parasites, but is thought to be an allergic response. Like people, dogs may be allergic to a variety of substances in their environment, and these may provoke an itchy skin response. In practice, however, it can be difficult to pinpoint the substance that provokes the allergy and even more difficult to avoid it. A dog that develops an irritated skin should be seen by a veterinary surgeon. Since these conditions can worsen quite rapidly, it is best if the dog receives prompt treatment, although it may take time for the condition to settle down and improve.

ehrlichiosis canine ehrlichiosis is a bacterial disease carried by ticks, which occurs in most tropical and subtropical countries. The bacteria are passed on in saliva after a tick bite and the dog becomes feverish and unwell. The disease may lead to HAEMORRHAGING and ANAEMIA, and in these cases the outcome is usually fatal.

electrocardiogram (ECG) a record of the changes in the heart's electrical activity, which is obtained by means of an instrument called an electrocardiograph. This is a DIAGNOSTIC TEST that may occasionally be recommended for a dog with a suspected heart disorder.

electroencephalogram (EEG) a record of the brain's electrical activity, which is obtained by means of an instrument called an electroencephalograph. This type of recording may occasionally be useful in diagnosing brain disorders in dogs. EEG recordings have shown that during the first two weeks of a puppy's life brain activity is at a very low level. By the age of four to five weeks, however, electrical activity is about the same as that of an adult dog.

'Elizabethan collar' a bucket-shaped device, looking rather like a lampshade, that is fitted over a dog's head and attached to its collar. It prevents the dog from scratching a sore ear or biting and interfering with a wound on any other part of its body. An Elizabethan collar can be obtained ready-made from a veterinary clinic or pet shop, but can also be made at home. A children's sand bucket with the base cut out is often suitable, as long as it is made of soft plastic. The edge that goes around the neck should be padded with sticking plaster to soften it, and strings fastened on to tie it to the dog's collar. Another alternative is to make the collar from a piece of strong card bent into a cone shape and trimmed to size.

An Elizabethan collar

Cut out the base and punch holes around the edge. Use adhesive tape to pad the edge and then tie the bucket to the collar, using string or lengths of tape or bandage.

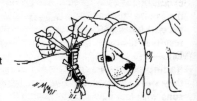

Elokomin fluke fever a disease that can occur in dogs in North America, which is caused by bacteria carried by parasitic flukes that inhabit fish such as trout and salmon. A dog may become infected if it eats raw fish containing the parasites, and the illness produces symptoms of DIARRHOEA and fever.

encephalitis inflammation of the brain. The word is sometimes used to describe symptoms affecting the nervous system that are associated with DISTEMPER.

encephalomyelitis inflammation of the brain and spinal cord that occurs uncommonly in dogs, usually as a complication of a rare viral disease called lymphocytic choriomeningitis. The virus is carried by mice, and if a dog is infected it usually develops feverish symptoms and is unwell for about a week before recovering. Occasionally, more severe symptoms may occur. Rarely, a person may become infected with the virus from a dog, which causes a slight feverish illness resembling 'flu. A much more likely source of infection, however, is house mice or even pet mice or hamsters.

entropion an eye condition seen particularly in spaniels and chow-chows in which one or both of the eyelids curls inwards and causes inflammation and irritation by rubbing on the eyeball. Ectropion, the opposite situation, also occurs, where the edge of the eyelid curls outwards and causes irritation by exposing the surface of the eye.

epiphora the condition in white dogs in which there is a wet, brownish-coloured streak running from each eye down the side of the nose because of an overflow of tears (lacrimal fluid). Lacrimal fluid is continually produced by tear glands in the eyes and is washed across the surface by the action of blinking. Normally, the excess drains away through the nasolacrimal duct, which runs from the eye into the nasal cavity. In some dogs, however, the ducts may become blocked for some reason or are poorly developed, and this results in the tears flowing down the face. (*See* ROUTINE CARE OF A DOG—Eye care, page 40.)

'fading puppy' syndrome fading puppies are so called because they sicken and die shortly after birth. There are a variety of reasons why this may occur, including congenital abnormalities and illnesses caused by bacteria (puppy septicaemia) and viruses (puppy viraemia). Among the bacteria that may be responsible are various strains of staphylococcus and streptococcus and the common gut bacterium, *E. coli*. Viruses that can cause severe illness and death include the DISTEMPER virus, canine adenovirus-1 and HERPES virus. Puppies may be infected after birth by an apparently healthy 'carrier' mother or another dog, and the situation is especially serious in breeding kennels. Strict standards of hygiene and good care of a bitch and her puppies helps to minimize the risks of infection.

false or **pseudo-pregnancy** a condition in a bitch following a period of 'heat' when symptoms of pregnancy develop although the animal has not been mated. If symptoms are severe or tend to recur, it is best to consult a veterinary surgeon and to consider having the bitch NEUTERED (*see* Sexual Behaviour and Breeding—Bitch, page 47).

fish hooks in areas where angling is popular it is not uncommon for dogs to get discarded fish hooks stuck into their skin. The barb on a hook makes it difficult to remove and it may be necessary to take the dog to a veterinary surgeon so that local ANAESTHETIC can be applied to lessen pain.

fits *see* CONVULSIONS.

fleas *see* PARASITES—External parasites, page 71.

fleshworm (*Dipetalonema reconditum*) a type of worm that occurs in some tropical and subtropical countries, which is passed on from one dog to another by the bite of fleas or lice.

flatulence dogs tend to be prone to attacks of flatulence, which can make them difficult to live with at times. This is usually related to the dog's diet, and the type of food being given should be looked at as a change may bring about an improvement. Various medications can be obtained from a veterinary surgeon, which may help to resolve this problem.

fomentations the application of hot fomentations to a wound or site of an abscess is an effective remedy that has stood the test of time. A fomentation consists of a pad of gauze, lint or cotton wool that has been soaked in hot water or a solution containing some substance, wrung out and then applied to a wound. The fomentation is applied for a few minutes at a time until it begins to cool and then is taken off and the process is repeated. It is best to continue for five or ten minutes and to repeat the process several times a day. Hot fomentations have the effect of increasing the supply of blood to an area of skin, which promotes healing of a wound or an AB-SCESS that has already burst. With a developing abscess, hot fomentations speed up the process of ripening so that it comes to a head more quickly. In the case of an abscess or where any kind of infection is involved, dissolving Epsom salts (magnesium sulphate) in the water makes the process even more effective. Fomentations can also be applied to relieve the pain of strained and sore muscles in dogs. This can be a useful form of treatment for various complaints in dogs, but it is best to consult a veterinary surgeon first to make sure that this is appropriate in each individual case.

foreign body, swallowed it is not uncommon for dogs, especially puppies and young animals, to pick up and swallow an inappropriate object. While these may sometimes pass through the gut and be eliminated with faeces without causing harm, this unfortunately is not always the case. An object may become stuck or cause an obstruction or perforation in some part of the gut with serious consequences. If it is known or even suspected that a dog has swallowed some object, it is wise to phone for veterinary advice. It may be necessary for the dog to have an X-ray to locate the object and a surgical operation to remove it, and this will almost certainly be necessary if the dog develops signs of illness.

fracture any break in a bone that may be complete or incomplete. In a simple (or closed) fracture, the skin remains more or less intact but in a compound (or open) fracture there is an open wound connecting the bone with the surface. This type of fracture is generally more serious as it provides a greater risk of infection and more blood loss. A 'greenstick fracture' occurs in a young animal whose bones are still soft and tend to bend rather than break. The fracture occurs on the opposite side to the causal force. A complicated fracture involves damage to surrounding soft tissue, including nerves and blood vessels. A depressed fracture involves the skull, when a piece of bone is forced inwards and may damage the brain.

It may or may not be obvious whether a dog has suffered a fracture, depending on the nature of the injury. Sometimes an X-ray is the only means of distinguishing between a fracture and DISLOCATION. Certain symptoms and signs of a fracture may be present. These include severe pain and swelling, an unusual degree of movement with a grating sound (crepitus), or there may be an obvious bump where a broken bone has been displaced. The pain and bleeding that may result from a fracture can easily lead to SHOCK. A dog that has suffered a fracture requires immediate veterinary treatment. Emergency treatment of broken bones is discussed under A–Z of First Aid for Dogs, *see* page 144.

frostbite frostbite is uncommon in dogs but can occur in those that are exposed to freezing temperatures for a long period of time or have been out in snow. Usually it is the extremities of the body that are affected, particularly the tips of the ears and tail, the paws, and the scrotum in small male dogs. The affected parts appear white or pale and feel and remain cold, with a loss of sensation. The skin may also seem swollen, dry and scaly, and in extreme cases affected parts may turn black and there is a risk of the development of GANGRENE. Veterinary advice should be obtained in cases of suspected frostbite but, as an interim measure, warm *but not hot* pads or towels can be applied to the affected parts. As the circulation returns, the skin usually reddens and will be painful for a time. The dog should be kept warm but neither should direct heat (hot-water bottles, hairdryers, etc) be applied nor the affected parts massaged as this can damage underlying tissues. If the skin starts to turn black rather than red it is best to take the dog to a veterinary surgeon immediately.

fungal diseases various species of fungus can be responsible for diseases in dogs, and some of these are more prevalent in countries other than Britain. One of the most common is RINGWORM, which is highly contagious and affects the skin. Fungal spores may be inhaled, ingested or enter through nicks in the skin and often cause symptoms affecting the nasal and respiratory passages, mouth, throat or skin, depending on the site of infection. Occasionally they can be responsible for more severe, systemic (whole body) illnesses in a dog.

gangrene death of tissue as a result of a loss of blood supply or bacterial infection. There are two types of gangrene, 'dry' and 'moist'. Dry gangrene is caused purely by a loss of blood supply, and the affected part becomes cold and then turns brown or black. There is an obvious line of demarcation between living and dead tissue, and eventually the gangrenous part is sloughed off. Most gangrene is caused by bacterial infection, and there is putrefaction and fluid leakage with an obnoxious smell. There is pain and fever, and without prompt surgical intervention and antibiotic treatment, bacterial toxins are absorbed into the bloodstream, leading to death from blood poisoning. Gangrene can occur in a dog as a result of injury, BURNS, FROSTBITE, etc, and is obviously more likely if treatment is delayed or in a dog that is a stray or otherwise neglected. It is always best to seek veterinary advice if in any doubt about the treatment of a wound or injury.

gastritis inflammation of the stomach lining (mucosa), causing discomfort and pain and possibly VOMITING. The condition may be caused by eating too much food too quickly, swallowing an irritating substance or by bacterial infection. If the symptoms persist or the dog shows obvious signs of becoming ill or dehydrated, veterinary attention should be sought.

gingivitis inflammation of the gums. This is usually caused by a build-up of tartar on the teeth at their junction with the gums, which enables bacteria to proliferate and attack the tissues. The gums may become red, swollen and irritated and bleed easily. If the tartar is not removed at this stage, the situation worsens and the gums may continue to swell and pull away from the root of the teeth. Bacteria are then able to attack the socket of the teeth, causing them to become loose and leading to severe infection or abscesses and great pain. The build-up of tartar should be prevented by giving the dog plenty of hard materials to chew and by cleaning the teeth. (*See* ROUTINE CARE OF A DOG—Cleaning teeth, page 39.)

glaucoma a painful disorder caused by pressure from a build-up of fluid within the eye, which can result in BLINDNESS. In dogs this tends to be an inherited condition particularly affecting basset hounds and cocker spaniels. Treatment may require specialized surgery on the eyeball.

grass-eating many dogs are in the habit of eating a small amount of grass from time to time, and this usually provokes retching and vomiting. It would seem that they do this to provide relief from some sort of digestive discomfort, and some dogs are more prone to this habit than others.

Griseofulvin an effective anti-fungal drug used in the treatment of ringworm (*see* PARASITES—Internal parasites, page 65).

haematoma a collection or leakage of blood that forms a firm swelling beneath the skin. It can arise anywhere as a result of a blow causing the rupture of a small blood vessel. In dogs, however, the most common site is on the ear flaps, arising as a result of head shaking or scratching, usually because of infestation with ear mites. Dogs with long, floppy ears, such as spaniels, are quite likely to develop a haematoma as they are more prone to ear troubles. The haematoma appears as a swelling that may alter in shape and is uncomfortable but not severely painful. Unless very small, the haematoma needs to be opened and drained or there will be a permanent distortion or 'cauliflower ear'. Hence a dog with this condition should be taken to a veterinary surgeon, and the operation will need to be performed under a general ANAESTHETIC.

haemophilia an hereditary disorder of blood coagulation that causes bleeding. It affects males with females being the carriers, and while it is better known in humans it can also affect dogs.

haemorrhage bleeding—a flow of blood from a ruptured blood vessel that may occur externally or internally. A haemorrhage is classified according to the type of vessels involved. Arterial haemorrhage is when bright red blood spurts in pulses from an artery. Venous haemorrhage is when there is a darker-coloured steady flow from a vein. In a capillary haemorrhage, blood oozes from torn capillaries at the surface of a wound. In addition, a haemorrhage may be primary, i.e. it occurs at the moment of injury. It is classed as reactionary when it occurs within 24 hours of an injury and results from a rise in blood pressure. Thirdly, a secondary haemorrhage occurs after a week or ten days as a result of infection (sepsis). Haemorrhage from a major artery is the most serious as large volumes of blood are quickly lost and death can occur within minutes. Haemorrhages at specific sites within the body are designated by special names, e.g. haematuria, from the kidney or urinary tract, often indicated by the presence of blood in the urine. Also, haemoptysis, bleeding from the lungs, indicated by the coughing up of blood, and haematemesis, from the stomach, which may be apparent if blood is vomited. (*See* A–Z OF FIRST AID—bleeding, page 141).

hardpad *see* DISTEMPER.

heart disease in common with human beings, dogs suffer from heart disease, which tends to be more common in older age. The form that this takes differs, however, in that dogs nearly always suffer from increasing weakness and failure of heart valves rather than the 'furring' of the pulmonary arteries that is so prevalent in people. In dogs it is usually the mitral valve that is involved, and this becomes enlarged and distorted so that the pumping action of the heart is less effective. Blood is able to leak back into the heart instead of being pumped around the body. The effects of this are progressive cardiac failure with symptoms of tiredness, breathlessness and noisy breathing, and coughing. At first, these symptoms are more apparent with exercise but as the condition worsens they can be detected even when the dog is resting. If the condition is severe, and particularly if it is left untreated, there may be a collection of fluid in the abdominal cavity, known as ascites. A dog with these symptoms requires veterinary attention, and various drugs are available that can help to control the condition and enhance the quality of life.

heart failure a failure of the heart to pump blood around the body, causing the dog to collapse and fight for breath. The gums appear a pale or white colour and the heartbeat is either very weak or cannot be detected. It is rare for this to arise suddenly in dogs, and some breeds have a genetic predisposition towards this condition. These include the very large breeds such as Dobermans and Great Danes and also Cavalier King Charles spaniels. Heart problems will usually have manifested themselves prior to sudden cardiac collapse. Heart failure is very serious and requires emergency first aid and veterinary treatment.

heartworm *see* PARASITES—Internal parasites, page 70.

heatstroke or **heat hyperpyrexia** a severe condition following exposure of the dog to excessive heat with a consequent rapid rise in its body temperature. The only mechanisms that the dog has to lower its temperature are panting and behavioural responses such as seeking out shade, drinking water or even lying in cool water. If the dog is confined in a hot, poorly ventilated place and has no access to water, its temperature regulation mechanisms are easily overcome and heatstroke may occur. It most commonly happens when a dog is left shut in a hot car in the summer and can occur even if a window is left open. Symptoms of heatstroke are firstly panting, drooling and anxiety, and the dog's gums turn to a bright red colour. The temperature rises to around 40.6°C (105°F) whereas it is normally about 38.5°C (101.5°F). If action is not taken, the temperature continues to rise, leading to collapse, coma, respiratory collapse (blue tinge to gums) and death. Owners should take care to prevent the possibility of overheating by making sure that dogs always have access to shade, cool surroundings and plenty of drinking water. It may be necessary to curtail exercise to short walks only or to cooler times of the day. Dogs with flattened faces, such as boxers, pugs, Pekinese, etc, are more at risk of heatstroke as their breathing is restricted. Also, breeds that naturally have a great deal of fur are more likely to suffer from overheating. Dogs should never be left in a car in warm or hot weather.

Heimlich's manoeuvre a procedure to dislodge a foreign body that is blocking the windpipe, causing choking. It was devised as an emergency procedure for choking in people but a manoeuvre identical in all respects can be used on a dog. (*See* A–Z OF FIRST AID, page 147.)

hepatitis *see* INFECTIOUS CANINE HEPATITIS.

hernia the protrusion of a greater or lesser part of an organ from out of its normal position in the abdominal cavity as a result of a weakness or rupture in restraining sheets of muscle. A congenital hernia is present at birth, and the most common one is an umbilical hernia, when a part of the intestine protrudes into the umbilical cord. This is caused by a failure of the abdominal wall muscles to close over beneath the umbilicus in a new-born puppy. A veterinary surgeon should be consulted and, unless very small, the hernia usually needs to be corrected by surgery.

An inguinal hernia occurs in bitches in the region of the lower abdomen or groin. A part of the bowel bulges through a weak part of the abdominal wall known as the inguinal canal. This type may start small but has a tendency to enlarge and normally requires corrective surgery, especially if there is any possibility of the bitch having puppies. Inguinal hernias are rare in male dogs but a scrotal hernia can develop in which a loop of intestine protrudes into the scrotum. Once again, the treatment is corrective surgery. A potentially more serious type of hernia can follow an accidental blow when the muscles of the diaphragm tear or rupture. Loops of intestine are able to bulge into the chest cavity, and this causes breathing difficulties, distress and to the dog being unable to lie down.

A perineal hernia is most common in an elderly male dog and

often arises as a result of an enlargement in the prostate gland that causes constipation and straining. There is a weakening of the muscles around the anus so that parts of the bowel are able to protrude, forming soft swellings. These may begin on one side but can enlarge to surround the anus, forming a swelling beneath the tail. This type of hernia can be difficult to treat surgically, and it is essential to prevent the dog from becoming constipated as any straining may cause further enlargement of the hernia.

herpes—canine herpes virus infection an uncommon but severe viral infection in puppies that is sometimes a cause of 'FADING PUPPY' SYNDROME. The virus is thought to cause few symptoms in adult dogs, but the illness is usually fatal in puppies and they may be born already dead. In other cases, they may be sickly at birth and fail to thrive or deteriorate soon afterwards, refusing to suckle and having symptoms of sickness, abdominal pain and distress.

hip dysplasia a developmental, inherited disease of the hip joints that particularly affects large breeds of dogs. About 20 per cent of German shepherds and retrievers have this condition. The socket or acetabulum in the hip (or innominate bone) is too shallow to accommodate fully the large upper leg bone or femur. In consequence, the bones are able to slip apart at the joint and they wear unevenly and so do not fit together properly. There is a range of severity with this disorder from mild to disabling, but a number of treatments are available to relieve the symptoms and make life more comfortable for the dog. In Britain, breeders of dogs susceptible to this problem normally have the hips of potential parents X-rayed to obtain a hip score. Dogs that have the condition can then be prevented from breeding as one means of trying to lessen the incidence of hip dysplasia.

hookworm *see* PARASITES—Other internal parasites, page 70.

hydrocephalus an abnormal collection of cerebrospinal fluid within the skull that causes a great increase in the size of the head in young puppies. Toy breeds that have a high, rounded head, such as the Chihuahua, seem to be more susceptible to this condition.

hyperthyroidism excessive activity of the thyroid gland or an overactive thyroid, resulting in an increased production of hormones. This may be caused by the presence of a tumour, and one sign in dogs is increased restlessness. The dog paces around and cannot settle and lie down, and this may be noticed particularly at night. Hyperthyroidism is a rare disorder in dogs.

hypochondria it is not unheard of for some dogs to feign illness or lameness in order to gain attention from humans. This is particularly likely to occur in an intelligent dog that has received a great deal of sympathetic attention for some real illness or injury in the past. The dog may sometimes try to solicit this lavish attention once again by exhibiting some of its previous symptoms. Of course, people may even reinforce this behaviour in the dog, for instance by asking it to 'show us your sore paw', or whatever the symptoms may be. The behaviour is more likely to occur in a dog that, rightly or wrongly, feels it is not receiving enough notice, for instance, one that is in a busy household with other dogs or pets. While a dog may be intelligent enough to try this strategy, it is not usually able to be consistent. It may show the symptoms only when other animals are being petted or when its owner is present and forget about them moments later. It is best to ignore the dog completely while it is behaving in this way but to give it plenty of praise for good behaviour at other times.

hypothermia the bodily state in which a dog's core temperature falls below 36.7°C (93°F) as a result of prolonged exposure to cold. At first, shivering occurs and the heart works harder to increase the flow of blood around the body. Eventually the shivering ceases, however, and with increasing chilling the function of the body organs becomes disturbed and cardiac output falls. The tissues require less oxygen as their functions start to fail, but eventually the heart is unable to supply even this reduced demand. The symptoms of hypothermia are, at first, shivering but then fatigue, lethargy, confusion, unconsciousness and convulsions. The dog's breathing is very shallow and slow, and the body feels cold to the touch. Death follows unless the dog is warmed and its core temperature is induced to rise. Any dog can develop hypothermia if it is out in cold, wet and windy weather for a prolonged period and cannot obtain shelter, particularly if it is injured or trapped and cannot move about. Dogs with thick fur are obviously better protected than those with a thin coat. Very young puppies and old dogs are also more vulnerable and should be protected from cold and damp. It is usually obvious if a dog is feeling cold as it will shiver and look miserable and will be happier with short walks and the protection of a coat in severe winter weather. A dog showing any signs of hypothermia needs immediate emergency first aid treatment.

hysteria in dogs, this term is applied to extreme behaviour that usually occurs before a convulsion in animals suffering from a particular type of brain disorder. The dog may rush around in a wild manner, knocking into objects and barking or howling, and may lose control of bowel and bladder functions. Eventually it may try to crawl into a dark space and either drops into an exhausted sleep or has convulsions. A dog in this state is not in control and is liable to bite. If possible, it should be shut into a darkened, confined space until the attack passes, and emergency veterinary help should be obtained. The dog should be closely watched and appropriate care given if convulsions occur. In some other situations, excitable or nervous dogs may exhibit extreme behaviour that is sometimes termed hysterical although there is no loss of control.

impotence inability of a male dog to perform the sexual act or to impregnate a bitch. There are many possible causes, including inflammation or infection of the penis, bladder or other organs, excessive matings, illness, exhaustion or debility, hormonal or other metabolic disorders. Obviously, this condition is usually only important in a valuable stud dog needed for breeding purposes. Stud dogs should not be used for breeding until they are at least one year old and not used regularly until the age of two.

incontinence (of urine) an inability to control urination so that there is a frequent dribbling of urine. True incontinence must be distinguished from inadequate house training, urination as a submissive response (usually seen in bitches) or immaturity. Urinary incontinence can have a variety of different causes, some of which are more common than others. In adult dogs, a frequent cause is inflammation, irritation or infection of the sphincter muscle, which controls the outlet of the bladder. This may arise because of the presence of stones or calculi somewhere in the urinary tract (*see* BLADDER STONES) or be caused by a bacterial infection. Both sexes can develop urinary stones and some breeds, e.g. dachshunds, Dalmatians and corgis, are particularly prone to this condition. Bacterial infections are more likely to occur in bitches, which have a much shorter urethra than male dogs, allowing easier access for organisms to the bladder and urinary tract. Incontinence arises in about 10 per cent of spayed bitches and may occur as a result of the rearrangement of internal organs. However, it is sometimes caused by a lack of female sex hormones, which cease to be produced once the reproductive organs are taken out. In these cases, the incontinence improves with hormone replacement therapy. Occasionally urinary incontinence is the result of some congenital defect during the development of a puppy and is present at birth. Usually this affects the ureters, which are a pair of fine tubes that carry urine from the kidneys to the bladder. This condition can sometimes be corrected by surgery.

infectious canine hepatitis (ICH) or **Rubarth's disease** this sometimes severe, infectious disease is caused by a virus designated Canine Adenovirus Type 1, or CAV-1. When ingested or swallowed, the virus may cause hepatitis, but if it is inhaled it can be one of the organisms responsible for KENNEL COUGH. There is a great range in the severity of the symptoms of ICH. At its most mild it may pass unnoticed, with the dog developing immunity to further attacks, but severe cases may have a fatal outcome. It is believed to be a common infection among dogs that have not been vaccinated, with the severest symptoms arising in young animals less than one year old. The virus attacks the liver, causing symptoms of inflammation (hepatitis). These include abdominal pain, fever, restlessness and the inability to lie down without distress. In about one-third of affected dogs jaundice develops, which is indicated by a yellowing of the eyelids, gums and skin and a deepened colour of urine. There is a swelling of lymph nodes and glands and internal haemorrhaging as a result of the virus damaging the walls of blood vessels, causing anaemia. Dogs with these severe symptoms develop a great thirst but refuse food, lose weight and become lethargic. In about one-fifth of dogs that survive and recover, a characteristic change occurs in the eye, the cornea becoming bluish-coloured and opaque in appearance. This condition, called 'blue eye', is usually short-lived, but a more serious and long-lasting effect is believed to occur in some dogs, and this is chronic kidney damage. Fortunately, infectious canine hepatitis can be prevented by vaccination.

intestinal obstruction and intussusception an obstruction in some part of the digestive tract is usually caused by the dog swallowing some inappropriate substance or foreign body. It can also occur in a dog that has eaten a bone, as fragments may combine together to form a hard indigestible mass, causing an obstruction within the intestine. This usually causes the dog to become very constipated and uncomfortable. Signs of obstruction include pain, vomiting, diarrhoea or constipation, and the dog should be seen by a veterinary surgeon.

intussusception a condition in which one length of the bowel slips inside an adjacent part beside or beneath it, much as a telescope closes up. This produces a double thickness and may lead eventually to a complete obstruction with symptoms of abdominal pain, fever and flatulence. This is a serious condition, and the dog will appear to be obviously unwell and in distress. An operation is necessary in order to save its life, and if this condition is suspected, a dog should be taken immediately to a veterinary surgeon.

jaundice a condition characterized by the unusual presence of bile pigment (bilirubin) in the blood, which is normally indicative of some form of liver disorder. With jaundice, bile, which is produced in the liver and stored in the gall bladder, passes into the blood instead of the intestines and because of this there is a yellowing of the skin and mucus membranes. This is particularly noticeable in the first instance in the lining of the lower eyelids. A further indication in dogs is that the urine turns a strong yellow or brown colour because of the presence of the pigment. There are two types of jaundice. Obstructive jaundice is caused by bile not reaching the intestine because of a blockage of the bile duct. In dogs, this can be caused by parasitic worm infestation, although this is rare, (*see* PARASITES—Internal Parasites, page 65) or the presence of a tumour. Non-obstructive jaundice is caused by various disorders and diseases, resulting in inflammation and damage of the liver. These include the swallowing of poisonous or toxic substances, INFECTIOUS CANINE HEPATITIS and LEPTOSPIROSIS. Jaundice should always be regarded seriously and the dog taken to a veterinary surgeon so that the cause can be investigated.

kennel cough, canine respiratory disease (CRD) or **infectious tracheobronchitis** an infectious, unpleasant cough, which has acquired its name because it most commonly occurs when large numbers of dogs from different places are brought together, as in animal rescue centres and boarding kennels. Most infected dogs exhibit the symptoms of the disease for about two or three weeks and then make a good recovery. In some animals, however, complications that can be fatal, such as pneumonia or severe bronchitis, may develop, especially in an old dog or puppy or one that already has some other illness. There are four main causal organisms responsible for kennel cough, the most prevalent of which is a bacterium, *Bordetella bronchiseptica*. As well as a cough, which may be severe, the dog frequently has a thick nasal discharge containing pus. Other causes of kennel cough are the canine adenoviruses 1 and 2 (CAV-1 and CAV-2) and parainfluenza virus, which cause symptoms of varying degrees of severity. Other viruses, especially mycoplasma, herpes virus and reovirus, may exacerbate the severity of the symptoms in some cases.

It is now possible for dogs to be vaccinated against the four main causative organisms of kennel cough, although protection lasts for a relatively short period of time, i.e. six months. Hence dogs that are regularly placed in boarding kennels should be vaccinated twice a year, and many establishments insist on seeing an up-to-date vaccination certificate before an animal is admitted. It is also the case that any natural immunity built up by a dog following an attack of kennel cough does not last for very long and the animal may have recurrent bouts of illness. The infection is also very contagious and likely to spread, so infected animals should be isolated.

kidney disease acute inflammation of the kidneys (nephritis) generally arises because of infection with the bacterium *Leptospira canicola*, a cause of one form of LEPTOSPIROSIS. This form of kidney disease usually occurs in younger dogs and causes fever, back pain, sickness and weight loss. Older dogs may suffer a gradual and progressive degeneration of the kidneys so that these are no longer able to filter waste products efficiently from the blood. These products are toxic at high levels in the blood, and the symptoms include fever, extreme thirst, vomiting, fatigue and, eventually, ulcers in the mouth. The dog usually passes considerable quantities of pale-coloured urine, which contains a protein substance called albumin. In cases of extreme kidney failure there is a build-up of the waste substance urea in the blood (uraemia). Early kidney disease in dogs can be greatly helped by treatment with various drugs and modification of the diet. If symptoms are severe, it is kinder to have the dog humanely put to sleep to avoid further suffering. A dog with any symptoms of kidney disorder should always be examined and treated by a veterinary surgeon.

kidney worm *see* PARASITES—Other internal parasites, page 70.

lameness lameness is a common affliction in dogs, caused either by some condition affecting a paw or one of the legs. In the course of daily activity the paws are susceptible to being hurt by sharp objects, and they should be checked regularly for signs of damage. Lameness can also be caused by a number of conditions affecting the limbs, including an injury of some kind, muscular strain or arthritis. Lameness is usually accompanied by pain, and unless the cause is over-exercise, which normally disappears with rest, it is best to take the dog to a veterinary surgeon for examination.

laparotomy a general term for a surgical procedure in which an incision is made in the abdomen under general ANAESTHETIC. Sometimes an instrument is inserted in order to obtain a sample of tissue for laboratory investigation (biopsy). Also, a laparotomy incision is necessary for various abdominal operations, such as neutering or spaying of a bitch.

leptospirosis an acute infectious disease caused by bacteria belonging to the genus Leptospira. There are two species of bacteria responsible for infections in dogs. *Leptospira canicola* is the most common and dogs are the normal reservoir hosts for this organism. At its worst, the infection can produce symptoms of diarrhoea, vomiting, fever, pain in the abdomen, kidney damage, loss of weight and death. It is believed, however, that in many dogs the infection passes unnoticed, producing few, if any, symptoms. Rarely, the bacteria can be responsible for an illness in people, which is called canicola fever.

Leptospira icterohaemorrhagiae is transmitted by rats, which are the main reservoir hosts, and it causes an illness in dogs that can result in serious liver damage. This organism is also dangerous to people, causing the serious and sometimes fatal illness Weil's disease. In dogs, symptoms of the illness are the same as those described above but additionally there is jaundice. Also, there may be small haemorrhages that show as pinpricks of bleeding in the mucous membranes of the eyes and mouth.

Unfortunately, dogs, rats and other mammals that have been infected or are carriers continue to excrete the organisms in their urine for a long time. The bacteria remains active even longer if excreted in water. Both people and dogs can be infected through cuts and skins abrasions if they are in contact with contaminated water. Dogs are obviously vulnerable to infection from their habit of sniffing and licking urine left by other dogs. It is important for both dogs and people not to swim or bathe in potentially contaminated water, particularly if it is still or stagnant and where rats are likely to be present. In general, people most at risk from Weil's disease are those who work on farms or at sewage plants.

Both forms of leptospirosis in dogs are prevented by routine vaccination.

lick granuloma a thickness of shiny tissue that can occur over the surface of a wound that has not been able to heal properly because of a dog's continual licking. It is important to try to prevent a dog from licking a wound as this delays and interrupts healing, may dislodge stitches and result in the formation of a thickened mass of scar tissue. (*See* ELIZABETHAN COLLAR).

lung fluke an internal parasite of some dogs in parts of South Africa and the USA. This parasite, *Paragonomus kellicotti*, has larval stages in crayfish and water snails. It usually infects stray dogs that scavenge on shorelines and causes coughing and irritation of the airways.

lungworm *see* Parasites—Other internal parasites, page 70.

lymphocytic choriomeningitis *see* ENCEPHALOMYELITIS.

mad itch *see* PSEUDO-RABIES.

mammary tumours *see* CANCER.

mange *see* Parasites—External parasites, page 74.

meningitis inflammation of the meninges (membranes) surrounding the brain and spinal cord. In dogs, it may arise as a result of a viral infection called lymphocytic choriomeningitis (see ENCEPHALOMYELITIS).

metritis inflammation and infection of the womb, which generally occurs after a bitch has had a litter of puppies. This is a potentially severe and life-threatening condition, producing symptoms of restlessness, fever, anxiety, loss of appetite and usually a foul-smelling discharge that may be bloodstained. A bitch that shows any of these symptoms after whelping requires urgent veterinary treatment and antibiotics to treat the infection. (See LABOUR AND BIRTH—When to intervene or call a vet, page 56).

milk fever see ECLAMPSIA.

mites see PARASITES—External parasites, page 73.

myasthenia gravis a serious and chronic condition of uncertain cause that causes weakening of skeletal and respiratory muscles. It is believed to be an autoimmune disease and, while usually associated with humans, can also affect dogs.

mycoplasma bacteria that may cause respiratory tract infections in dogs and are implicated in some cases of KENNEL COUGH.

nettlerash an allergic reaction in an individual exposed to some substance to which he or she is hypersensitive in which the response is manifested on the skin. Raised red patches develop that may last for some hours, and there can be irritation, discomfort and itching. It can be very difficult to discern the cause, but insect stings, household chemicals, detergents, shampoos, soaps and flea collars, etc, have all been implicated. There can be swelling of the skin on the head, ears, throat and gums, which can be unpleasant and cause the dog considerable discomfort. The symptoms may subside after an hour or two but can recur. The dog should be taken to a veterinary surgeon and will usually be treated with antihistamine, which brings a rapid improvement in symptoms.

neuralgia pain in some part of, or following the course of, a nerve and its branches. Neuralgic pain is acute and severe, and in dogs it may sometimes affect muscles and nerves in the region of the shoulders and neck. The dog should be examined by a veterinary surgeon and will usually require drug treatment to relieve symptoms.

neutering a surgical operation to remove the reproductive organs of a dog in order to prevent mating and breeding. In male dogs this operation (also called castration) involves the removal of the testicles. In bitches, neutering, spaying or ovariohysterectomy involves the surgical removal of the womb and ovaries. Since the reproductive organs are completely removed, the sex hormones that they secrete and are responsible for sexual behaviour are no longer present, and this modifies the dog's behaviour. In both sexes, this usually means that the dog no longer shows any sexual interest but occasionally, especially in a male that has been mated in the past, this behaviour has become conditioned and persists. The problem can be improved by behavioural modification training and hormone (progestagen) treatment. Neutering of male dogs is often carried out to alter behaviour, i.e. to remove inappropriate sexual behaviour, straying or territorial marking with urine in the home. It reduces these tendencies in most dogs and often makes them less aggressive towards other males. Also, a male dog that has shown these tendencies may also have been a dominant animal and difficult to train. Neutering often improves this, making the animal more docile and easier to control. A neutered male dog cannot develop a tumour on a testicle and is less likely to suffer an enlargement of the prostate gland in older age.

In bitches, neutering removes all aspects of sexual behaviour and any possibility of unwanted litters of puppies. It has no apparent effect on other behaviour and does not alter the character of the bitch. Neutered bitches cannot develop womb infections (pyometra) and the risk of mammary tumours (*see* CANCER) is greatly reduced. If the bitch is neutered before coming into season for the first time, there is no risk of the development of such a tumour. About 10 per cent of bitches who have this operation develop problems of urinary incontinence in middle or older age. In a proportion of these cases, this is caused by a lack of oestrogen and can be successfully treated with hormone replacement therapy. Neutered dogs are more likely to become obese, but this can be controlled by reducing the amount of food offered or by feeding a 'light' diet.

obesity the accumulation of excess fat in the body, mainly in the subcutaneous tissues (beneath the skin), caused by eating more food than is necessary to produce the required energy for each day's activity. A dog is considered obese if its ribs cannot easily be felt, and this is more common in bitches and in middle-aged and elderly dogs of both sexes. Bitches naturally have a greater proportion of body fat, which perhaps explains why they are more likely to become obese. After neutering, both bitches and dogs are more likely to lay down body fat and become obese and, usually, adjustments in the diet are necessary to prevent this from happening.

A recent survey has shown that in the United Kingdom there are a greater number of obese dogs and cats than in any other European country. In Britain, about half of all dogs are obese, and two out of three spayed bitches become too fat. Surveys have shown that obese dogs are more likely to have overweight owners, particularly if the latter are middle-aged or elderly. Some breeds are more prone to becoming too fat, e.g. cocker spaniels, pugs and Labradors.

In common with people, obesity poses a threat to the health and wellbeing of a dog. It shortens life expectancy, and the dog runs an increased risk of developing various diseases and disorders, including heart disease, DIABETES mellitus, breathing and respiratory problems, joint and skeletal disorders such as ARTHRITIS, and poorer immunity to infections. An obese bitch is more likely to suffer problems in giving birth to puppies. Skin disorders, susceptibility to heat stroke, irritability and snappiness are all more likely in an obese dog. Also, a fat dog is at greater risk of death if it has to be given a general anaesthetic.

To help it lose weight, the dog should be given less food and, preferably (as long as there is no underlying disorder), a gradually increased amount of exercise. It may be best to consult a veterinary surgeon so that the dog's target weight can be established and advice obtained on the type and amount of food to give. Commercial dog food manufacturers and feeding specialists now produce a variety of 'light' diets for dogs, and one of these may prove to be the best solution. Some of these foods have the advantage that they can still be given in reasonable amounts (so the dog does not feel continually hungry) but are weight-reducing as they contain less fat and more fibre. Of course, no extra feeding in the form of titbits should be given to an obese dog. Once a dog has reached its target weight, and usually this takes some weeks, the situation can be reviewed. A little more food (usually about 20 per cent) can then be given to maintain the dog at its correct weight, although some adjustments may be needed from time to time.

oedema an accumulation of fluid in the body, possibly beneath the skin or in cavities or organs. In the case of an injury, the swelling may be localized but can be more general as in kidney or heart failure and liver disease.

oestrus cycle the reproductive cycle of a bitch in which she is sexually receptive and able to mate and become pregnant. (*See* SEXUAL BEHAVIOUR AND BREEDING—Bitch, page 47).

orchitis inflammation and infection of a testicle that may occur as a result of an injury. The dog should be taken to a veterinary surgeon and is likely to require treatment with antibiotics.

orthopaedic surgery surgery to repair fractured limb and hip bones or to treat ligament injuries and problems with intervertebral discs, quite commonly carried out on dogs. As in human medicine, a greater range of advanced surgical procedures is now available to treat bone and joint disorders in dogs.

osteoarthritis *see* ARTHRITIS.

otitis externa *see* EAR INFLAMMATION.

ovulation the point during the oestrous cycle when eggs are released from the ovaries of a bitch. (*See* SEXUAL BEHAVIOUR AND BREEDING—Bitch, page 47).

parainfluenza canine parainfluenza virus is one of the causal organisms of KENNEL COUGH in dogs. They can be protected from this infection by vaccination.

paralysis a condition ranging from muscle weakness to total loss of muscle movement and sensation caused by disease or damage to the brain, spinal cord or an individual nerve pathway. Paralysis in dogs usually results either from injury, disease and degeneration of the intervertebral discs of the back, infection, especially DISTEMPER, or poisoning. Posterior paralysis, affecting the hind quarters and back legs, is the most common form in dogs. If it arises as a result of distemper, the paralysis tends to get progressively worse and the dog usually has to be put to sleep. This type of paralysis may arise as a result of disease affecting the intervertebral discs, and long-backed breeds such as corgis and dachshunds are especially prone to this. If the paralysis is severe, i.e. there is a complete loss of sensation, the dog is also likely to be incontinent. The animal may attempt to drag itself around using its front legs and is likely to develop pressure sores ('bedsores'), a situation that is made worse by the leakage of urine. The dog needs to have a soft surface on which to lie, and must be kept clean and turned over frequently to try and ease the problem. Treatment for the paralysis will depend on the nature of the condition and the likely outcome. The dog may need a prolonged period of rest combined with drug treatment (corticosteroid hormones) or surgery if this is feasible. In other cases, it may be necessary and kinder to have a dog put to sleep.

An inherited disorder that causes abnormalities in the vertebrae in the region of the neck can affect some larger breeds of dog such as Great Danes. The deformed vertebrae press on the spinal cord, and this causes some degree of paralysis of the front limbs resulting in unsteadiness ('wobbler syndrome').

A dog may suffer paralysis of a front limb as a result of an accidental injury that damages the radial nerve. This is called radial paralysis and often results from a shoulder injury. If the nerve is badly damaged and unlikely to recover, it is usually necessary for the limb to be amputated as it becomes susceptible to injury, infection and gangrene. Although it looks ungainly, most dogs are adaptable and learn to get about quite well on three legs if they have to.

parvovirus one of a group of small viruses, responsible for a severe illness in dogs called canine parvovirus infection. This disease is relatively recent in that it was unknown in dogs before 1978. In that year, however, the illness manifested itself in various countries, and there have been repeated outbreaks ever since. A related virus in cats, called feline panleukopenia virus, responsible for the illness feline infectious enteritis, was already in existence, and there is evidence that the canine form arose from this by mutation. It is believed that the mutant canine virus somehow became established in a manufactured product used for dogs. Since it first arose, however, the virus has become a significant threat to the health of dogs, responsible for severe illness and death, particularly in puppies and young animals. It is a highly contagious infection passed in the faeces of an infected dog but able to persist for a long time on the ground and resistant to many chemical treatments. Hence direct contact is not necessary for the disease to spread, and the virus is difficult to eradicate once present. The virus causes two types of illness, the most common being a form of gastroenteritis in puppies after weaning. The illness usually begins with lethargy and vomiting and is followed by severe diarrhoea, which may be liquid and contain blood. The dog rapidly becomes dehydrated and may soon collapse and die. Treatment is by means of fluids given intravenously but in 10 per cent of cases there is a fatal outcome.

A much rarer form of infection causes inflammation and damage to heart muscle (myocarditis), and this occurs in younger puppies before weaning. An infected bitch passes on the virus to her puppies during pregnancy or soon after birth. Usually, the puppies appear to be healthy at first but begin to sicken and die suddenly around the age of three to six weeks. The puppies shown symptoms of heart failure and respiratory collapse, and, commonly, the infection kills about two-thirds of the litter. Those that survive have damaged hearts and are likely to suffer ill health in adult life as a consequence of the infection.

Adult dogs exposed to parvovirus seem to be more resistant, with a fatal outcome in only 1 per cent of cases. Fortunately, an effective vaccine has been developed that protects dogs against parvovirus infection, but outbreaks occur from time to time in unvaccinated dogs in most parts of the world.

pathogen a term applied to an organism that causes disease. Most disease-causing pathogens affecting dogs are bacteria or viruses. However, pathogens can be present in or on the body of a dog without causing symptoms of illness. The animal is then a 'carrier' of the pathogen and poses a risk to other dogs as a potential source of infection.

periodontal disease disease of the gums (*see* ROUTINE CARE OF A DOG—Cleaning teeth, page 39).

Perthe's disease a disease of the hip affecting the head of the femur, the long bone of the thigh. It occurs in children aged between four and ten, but an identical condition also occurs in young dogs.

There is inflammation, pain and lameness caused by various changes that occur in the bone. In children, the condition is treated by prolonged rest, traction and splinting of the limb. In dogs, treatment is usually aimed at relieving the symptoms, and normally the condition resolves as the animal matures. Initial diagnosis is made with the aid of X-rays.

plaster cast a dog that FRACTURES the lower part of a limb may need to have the leg immobilized in plaster while the bone heals. Plaster casts are not an ideal solution for dogs as they tend to get wet, chewed or dislodged in some way. Modern synthetic materials can be used and have many advantages, including lighter weight and increased durability, but the cost of these may be prohibitive.

pleurisy inflammation of the pleura, the membranes that cover the lungs and line the inside of the chest wall. It is a severe and painful condition that is usually a complication of pneumonia when it occurs in dogs. There is pain when breathing, which tends to be rapid and shallow, fever and loss of appetite. A dog with this condition is likely to need specialist nursing and hospital care.

pneumonia an infection of the lungs resulting in inflammation with the small air sacs becoming filled with pus and fluid. In dogs it is quite an unusual condition and usually connected with a bacterial infection arising as a result of a disease such as distemper. The symptoms are painful breathing, fever and loss of appetite. The dog needs veterinary treatment with antibiotics and rest, and should be kept warm and comfortable.

poisoning each year veterinary surgeons have to try to treat a number of dogs that have been poisoned, and often these distressing occurrences could be prevented with a little more thought and care. The majority of cases involve dogs eating toxic substances, but less commonly poisoning may be through inhalation of toxic fumes. It is extremely rare for poisons to be absorbed through the skin. Usually, if the dog has a toxic substance on its coat, the poison is ingested when the dog licks and cleans its fur.

As with children, most dogs that are poisoned are very young, although this is not invariably the case. Most people are aware of the risk of accidental poisoning when there are small children in the home. The same care needs to be taken in a household with a dog, and any potentially harmful substance should be kept in an inaccessible place. Many substances have been the cause of poisoning in dogs. These include household chemicals, paints, detergents and cleaners, garden products such as weedkillers, slug pellets and insecticides, rodenticides, e.g. Warfarin, strychnine, a number of poisonous plants, many of which are commonly grown, prescription drugs and illegal substances. Also, insecticidal products that are used directly on the dog, such as a flea collar that is eaten. Tar, oil, petrol and antifreeze containing ethylene glycol may all cause poisoning if ingested. The symptoms of poisoning vary according to the nature of the substance. Corrosive substances such as household and DIY chemicals and petrol cause internal BURNS, fluid loss and SHOCK (*see* A–Z OF FIRST AID, page 150). Other poisons may cause ABDOMINAL PAIN, DIARRHOEA and VOMITING, breathing difficulties, neurological symptoms, CONVULSIONS or PARALYSIS, listlessness, COMA and collapse. If it is known or suspected that a dog has been poisoned, veterinary advice should immediately be obtained, and it may be necessary to give emergency first aid. As much information as possible should be obtained about the poison, such as a sample or the container it came in, as this will aid the veterinary surgeon in giving treatment to counteract its effects.

pregnancy *see* SEXUAL BEHAVIOUR AND BREEDING, page 51.

progressive retinal atrophy (PRA) a gradual deterioration in vision caused by a progressive degeneration of the light-sensitive layer of the eye, the retina. This condition can assume one of two different forms. There is either a general deterioration over the whole of the retina or else the centre is affected first so that the dog fails to see objects that are straight ahead. Some breeds are more prone to the first form, e.g. Irish setters and poodles, and others to the second type, e.g. golden retrievers and Labradors. Collies can be affected by a similar condition, called collie eye anomaly, which is inherited. Efforts are being made to eradicate this disorder by not breeding from affected animals.

prolapsed eyeballs breeds that have naturally protruding eyeballs, such as pugs and Pekinese, are vulnerable to this condition. The eye sockets are so shallow that an eyeball can become completely displaced. This can occur as a result of the dog being held firmly by the scruff of the neck or following a fight or some other trauma. The dog needs immediate veterinary attention as the eye should be put back in place as soon as possible. The veterinary surgeon may advise covering the prolapsed eyeball with a clean pad of suitable material soaked in cold water until expert assistance is available.

protozoal diseases diseases that can affect dogs (and other mammals), the cause of which are micro-organisms called protozoa. The most important one in dogs is TOXOPLASMOSIS, but there are a number of others that occur mainly in countries with warm climates.

prostate gland a gland in the male reproductive system that is situated below the bladder, opening into the urethra, and beneath the rectum. The prostate gland produces and secretes a fluid that carries sperm when the dog mates with a bitch. A common problem in older dogs is enlargement of the gland, which can cause interference with urination and defecation. This usually responds to hormone treatment but surgical castration (NEUTERING) may prove necessary. Occasionally, the prostate gland is the site of a tumour and this is the cause of the enlargement. Treatment for this will probably involve surgery, and unfortunately the outlook is not very hopeful for growths that are cancerous.

prostagens synthetic chemical preparations resembling the natural hormone progesterone. They may be given to bitches to treat the symptoms of false or pseudo-pregnancy (*see* SEXUAL BEHAVIOUR AND BREEDING—Bitch, page 47) or for contraception. In male dogs, they may be given to try to prevent scent marking with urine and inappropriate sexual mounting. In both dogs and bitches, progestagen therapy can help to control the tendency to roam. These hormones are normally used for as short a period as possible.

pseudo-pregnancy or pseudo-cyesis *see* SEXUAL BEHAVIOUR AND BREEDING, page 50.

pseudo-rabies or **Aujesky's disease** an unpleasant viral disease affecting dogs, which occasionally occurs in most parts of the world, especially where pig-rearing is common. Dogs contract the virus from eating under-cooked pork, and the illness usually has a fatal outcome. The disease is short and intense, beginning about ten days after infection. At the beginning of the illness, the dog becomes highly excited and barks excessively, frothing at the mouth because of increased salivation. It develops a severe itch in the head region or elsewhere and worries this constantly, making the skin raw and bleeding. This is called 'mad itch', which is another popular name for this illness. After the period of excitement the dog becomes lethargic, loses coordination and becomes progressively paralysed until it eventually falls into a coma and dies. There is a superficial resemblance to rabies but the disease is of shorter duration.

pyometra inflammation and infection of the uterus or womb arising in the few weeks following the bitch's period of heat. This is quite a common condition, especially in a middle-aged animal, and requires emergency surgery in order to save the dog's life. Symptoms of pyometra include lethargy, excessive thirst, high temperature, vomiting and loss of appetite, and these symptoms can arise quite suddenly. The infection leads to a build-up of pus in the womb. In closed pyometra, the neck of the womb, or cervix, is blocked and the collection of pus causes swelling, which may be detected externally as a distended abdomen. In open pyometra, the cervical canal is open, allowing some of the pus to drain away to the outside as a discharge that the bitch may lick to clean away. Because of the accumulation of infected material, poisonous substances are absorbed into the bloodstream, which may cause shock and death from toxaemia. Alternatively, the uterus may rupture, again causing death from generalized infection. If any signs of illness are present in a bitch following a period of heat, she should be taken immediately to a veterinary surgeon. Treatment consists of surgical removal of the infected uterus (NEUTERING) along with a course of antibiotics to kill the infection. Of course, this means that the bitch can no longer have puppies but the operation is essential in order to save her life. If pyometra is suspected, the bitch should not be given anything to eat or drink as she will need a general anaesthetic. If pyometra is caught early and receives prompt attention, the dog can be expected to make a good recovery.

rabies an extremely severe viral disease that can affect people, dogs and many wild and domestic animals. Once symptoms are present, it is invariably fatal except in the case of one or two extremely rare exceptions. The normal route of transmission is through the bite of an infected (rabid) animal, the virus being present in saliva. It is possible, although more rare, for saliva to enter a cut or to be inhaled and for infection to occur in this way.

Both people and dogs can be vaccinated against rabies. However, vaccination is not permitted for dogs in Great Britain except in special circumstances, i.e. if they are going into quarantine kennels or abroad to a country where rabies is endemic. In some countries, e.g. most parts of the USA, vaccination against rabies is a legal requirement for owners of dogs and cats. The fate of a dog bitten by another animal that is proved to be rabid depends upon the country concerned and the vaccination status. The accepted recommendation is that a non-vaccinated animal should immediately be put to sleep. It may be possible for the dog to be treated with antiserum and rabies vaccine and kept strictly quarantined for a period of at least six months. A dog that has been vaccinated would usually be treated in a similar way and quarantined for at least three months. In western countries, it is rare for a person to be infected with rabies. Prompt treatment of any bite, by thorough cleansing of the wound, injections of rabies vaccine, antiserum and immunoglobulin can prevent the disease from developing.

A dog with rabies passes through three stages, and symptoms usually appear within four months, but it can be six months or longer. In the first stage there is a change in the nature of the dog. The animal may wish to hide away and seem fearful or it may become restless and run around barking. Alternatively, the dog becomes more affectionate than usual. This stage is short-lived, generally lasting for no more than two days. It is followed by a phase of great excitement and agitation, called 'furious' rabies, in which the dog usually rushes around biting at objects, other animals and people. The dog is sensitive to sounds and light, and if left free may run and run for miles snapping at anything in its path. If the dog is confined, it may chew at inappropriate materials with sufficient force to break its teeth. In the final stage, the dog becomes progressively more paralysed, this phase being called 'dumb' rabies. There is a characteristic change in the voice, which becomes husky because of effects on the throat muscles. Saliva drips from the mouth as the dog cannot swallow properly, and in general the animal appears as though it has something stuck in its throat. Some dogs suffer from CONVULSIONS during this stage and may die in the course of a fit. Others pass into a coma from which they do not recover. Without intervention, death normally occurs within five to ten days from the start of symptoms.

In those countries where rabies is endemic, which includes most of Europe, the virus persists in a variety of wild animals, including bats, foxes, skunks, coyotes and wolves. These animals are a potential source of infection for domestic pets, which can only be effectively protected if all are vaccinated. Unfortunately, it is always the case that some animals are not vaccinated and so rabies continues to pose a grave risk to the health of people and animals alike. This is the reason why vaccination is not permitted in Britain because it is feared that this would lead to a relaxation in people's attitude to rabies. Vigilant quarantine and other regulations governing the movement of animals have so far kept Britain free of the disease. It is necessary that this vigilance and high standard should be constantly maintained to ensure that this continues to be the case.

radiography the diagnostic technique of examining the body using X-rays. A radiograph is the image produced by X-rays on a film. For dogs, as for people, radiography is an important aid to diagnosis and a guidance in the treatment of a number of disorders and conditions. Examples include the diagnosis of fractures, screening for HIP DYSPLASIA and other skeletal conditions, and examination of tissues and organs following the injection of dyes to distinguish structures more easily. In certain circumstances it may be necessary to sedate a dog or to give a general ANAESTHETIC before using radiography as it is essential for the animal to remain perfectly still.

reovirus a virus that may contribute towards KENNEL COUGH in dogs.

respiration the whole process by which air is drawn into and out of the lungs during which oxygen is absorbed into the bloodstream and carbon dioxide and water are given off. External respiration is the actual process of breathing and the exchange of gases (oxygen and carbon dioxide) that takes place in the lungs. Internal respiration is the process by which oxygen is given up from the blood circulation to the tissues in all parts of the body and carbon dioxide is taken up to be transported back to the lungs. Respiration is essential for all life processes, and tissues and organs soon become unable to function if it ceases because of accident or illness.

The process of drawing air into the lungs is known as inhalation or inspiration, and expelling it out is known as exhalation or expiration. The rate at which this occurs is known as the respiratory rate, and this varies between different species of mammals. In a normal healthy dog, respiration should be easy and not noisy or laboured in any way. Obviously, in a dog that has been exercising hard or one that is hot, respiration is more noticeable and the animal pants and breathes at the same time. Dogs are subject to a number of respiratory and breathing disorders. If breathing is shallow, rapid, laboured or distressed in any way, it is a sign that something is wrong and the whole process of respiration may be in jeopardy. The dog should be taken to a veterinary surgeon for examination, diagnosis and treatment. In some circumstances, it may be necessary to give a dog ARTIFICIAL RESPIRATION (*see* A–Z OF FIRST AID, page 140).

rickets a malformation of the bones of young mammals caused by a deficiency of vitamin D. The disease is characterized by stunted growth and soft bones that bend out of shape and cause deformities. Bones are hardened by the deposition of calcium salts, and this cannot happen in the absence of vitamin D. Because of a much greater understanding of the nutritional needs of pregnant bitches and young puppies, rickets is now an extremely rare condition in dogs, at least in western countries.

ringworm a highly infectious disease that attacks the hairs and outer layers of dead skin and is readily transmitted from one mammal to another and to people. It is a fungal infection and the most common causal fungus in dogs is called *Microsporum canis*. Paradoxically, this fungus is even more at home on cats, which can form a reservoir of infection without necessarily exhibiting any symptoms. Ringworm typically appears as circular, bare skin lesions with raised, dry, crusted edges. However, the lesions may not be circular but just bare patches. The hair at the margins is normally brittle and breaks and falls out easily. The lesions may be itchy, but often this is not the case so scratching does not always occur. The bare patches tend to enlarge gradually as the condition spreads, and if scratching does occur, secondary bacterial infection may arise with the production of pus. Young mammals are thought to be more susceptible to ringworm because of their immature immune system.

A dog with a suspected ringworm infection must be examined and treated by a veterinary surgeon. It may be necessary to identify the fungus by examining hair samples under ultraviolet light. *Microsporum canis* emits a characteristic yellow-green fluorescence that is not given off by some other fungi that cause ringworm. Occasionally, samples of the fungus may be collected and cultured in a laboratory to identify the particular organism involved. Treatment has to be quite thorough and, because of the contagious nature of the infection, all pets and home surroundings should be included. It is preferable to burn all bedding and other items used by an infected dog, although strong disinfectants can also be used. The animal itself is treated with tablets containing antifungal drugs and fungicidal shampoos and lotions for the lesions. It may be necessary to continue with treatment for some time as the infection can be quite resistant. Fungal spores may persist for some years in the environment and are capable of producing a new infection.

People involved with an infected animal should take precautions, wear gloves, wash their hands and keep handling to a minimum. If a member of the family develops a skin irritation then he or she should seek medical advice. It is always better to treat ringworm promptly before it has a chance to spread.

road accidents *see* A–Z OF FIRST AID—broken bones and disclocations page 144.

roundworm *see* PARASITES—Internal parasites, page 66.

salivary glands three pairs of glands, parotid, submandibular and sublingual, that produce saliva. Occasionally a CYST may form, connected with the sublingual gland beneath the tongue, which is called a ranula.

scalds *see* A–Z OF FIRST AID, burns and scalds, page 145.

scurf scurf or dandruff may be present in a dog's coat and consists of flakes of dead, dry skin. Regular brushing helps to keep the problem under control, and very often an adjustment in the dog's diet or a vitamin and mineral supplement can help. A dog that has been neglected or is in poor condition often has scurf and a dull coat, but this usually soon improves with good feeding.

sedatives there are a number of circumstances in which it may be advisable for a dog to be given a sedative drug or tranquilliser. These include any circumstances in which the dog is very agitated, frightened or liable to bite, as is quite often the case when visiting the veterinary surgery. Some dogs need a sedative prior to travelling or being clipped, or one may be given to make a dog feel sleepy before it receives a general ANAESTHETIC.

self-mutilation there are a number of circumstances in which self-mutilation in the form of biting or scratching can take place. These include extreme itching, which is often caused by infestation with external parasites, particularly the sarcoptic mange mite, which causes canine scabies, and lice (*see* PARASITES—External parasites page 73). Other skin conditions such as ECZEMA can cause a degree of self-mutilation, as can some diseases. Among the latter are certain hormonal disorders and the viral disease PSEUDO-RABIES. A dog with any form of skin lesion should always be seen by a veterinary surgeon so that it can receive appropriate treatment and obtain relief.

shock a serious physiological condition of acute circulatory failure in which the blood pressure in the arteries is too low to provide the normal blood, and hence oxygen supply, to the body. There are very many causes of shock, including external or internal HAEMORRHAGE resulting from injuries or illness, diseases that cause VOMITING and DIARRHOEA, BURNS, POISONING, organ failure, ELECTROCUTION, ALLERGIC reaction to insect stings, and others. Shock is a life-threatening condition requiring emergency first aid and urgent veterinary treatment for an affected dog (*see* A–Z OF FIRST AID, page 150).

slipped disc or **prolapsed intervertebral disc** a very painful condition of the back that affects dogs as well as people and is more common in middle-aged animals. Some breeds are especially susceptible, and these include those with long backs and short legs, particularly corgis and dachshunds and also Cavalier King Charles spaniels. The intervertebral discs provide cushioning for the spinal cord and are composed of an outer, fibrous layer over a pulpy centre. A slipped disc is caused by the inner layer being pushed through the fibrous layer to impinge upon nerves, causing pain. The prolapse usually occurs during sudden twisting or bending of the backbone, for instance, when the dog jumps up. There is severe pain either in the neck or lower back (cervical or lumbar region). The dog may stand still and rigid because movement is so painful. There may be partial or total PARALYSIS of the front or hind quarters in severe cases. Treatment involves rest and giving pain-relieving drugs but surgery may sometimes be necessary.

snake bites *see* BITES.

spaying *see* NEUTERING.

stinging nettles dogs are not immune to the effects of stinging nettles and can experience severe responses. Dogs with thin coats or short hair are especially susceptible and there have been cases of death from shock. (*See* ANAPHYLACTIC SHOCK and A–Z OF FIRST AID—shock, page 150.)

stings *see* BEE AND WASP STINGS.

strabismus rarely, a dog may have a squint, or strabismus, so that each eye points in a different direction. There is often a fault in the muscles controlling the eyeballs, which may be congenital or inborn or arise as a result of accidental damage to the muscles or nerves that supply them.

strained muscles dogs can easily strain muscles through overexertion and usually this involves the limbs. The signs are a limp, indicating pain, and possibly swelling and discomfort when the affected part is touched. Usually the problem resolves with rest and restricted exercise for a few days. However, unless it is certain that over-exercise is the cause, it is wise to take the dog for veterinary examination in case there is some other underlying condition.

stress it is recognized that dogs can suffer from stress, anxiety and insecurity, which are usually manifested in a change in behaviour. The dog may refuse food, wet the floor or even develop physical symptoms such as DIARRHOEA as a result of stress. Usually, problems can be overcome with care and attention from the dog's owners. The benefits of psychiatric counselling for dogs are controversial, but this treatment is becoming increasingly popular in the USA.

sunburn sunburn is not usually a problem in dogs as they will normally seek shade before any harm is done. Thin-coated, and especially white, dogs may be at risk and may need to be kept indoors with vulnerable areas such as the nose protected with a sunscreen preparation.

superfecundation the situation in which the puppies in a single litter have different fathers because their mother mated with more than one dog during her fertile heat period. (*See* SEXUAL BEHAVIOUR AND BREEDING, page 49).

tail docking the amputation of a greater or lesser part of the tail, which was formerly carried out on many breeds of pedigree dog for the purposes of showing. The original purpose was supposedly to prevent the tail of a hunting dog from being trapped, caught up or injured while the animal was working. Eventually, however, many dogs had their tails routinely docked whether they were used for hunting or not. The British Veterinary Association has been opposed to the practice for many years, and recently it has been discontinued and made illegal. The only legitimate reason for amputation of the tail is in the event of severe injury.

tail injuries since a dog's tail is long and highly mobile it is quite prone to accidental injury and damage. These injuries include FRACTURES, DISLOCATIONS, wounds, cuts and even severing of the tip of the tail. In some dogs, chronic BLEEDING and sores can affect the tail. As with any other type of injury, veterinary attention is needed and emergency first aid may be required. Sometimes amputation of a severely damaged tail may be necessary.

tapeworms *see* PARASITES—Internal parasites, page 68.

tartar a substance that can build up on the teeth of a dog leading to decay. (*See* ROUTINE CARE OF A DOG—Cleaning teeth, page 39).

temperature a dog's temperature is usually taken by gently inserting a thermometer into the rectum. A normal temperature is usually around 38.5°C (101.5°F) except in two uncommon breeds of dog, the Chinese crested and Mexican hairless, in which it is 40.7°C (105.5°F). As in people, a rise in temperature, except when the dog is naturally hot, is often a sign that something is wrong and may indicate the onset of an illness. A persistently high temperature of 39.4°C or above indicates a fever, and it is wise to seek veterinary attention to try to determine the cause. A lowered temperature of 37.2°C or below is also a cause for concern and the dog needs to be covered and kept warm until expert help can be obtained.

tetanus an infectious disease with the common name lockjaw, caused by the bacterium *Clostridium tetani*, which lives in the soil. Dogs are much less likely to contract this disease than people, in whom it is serious and sometimes fatal. Spores of the bacteria enter through a wound, especially one that is deep and penetrating, and the organism proliferates, producing toxins. These toxins cause muscular spasms and paralysis, and when the respiratory muscles are involved, death may occur by asphyxia. Early signs of tetanus in dogs include increased intolerance to noise and light, stiffening of muscles and protrusion of the haws, or third eyelids. It is possible to give dogs VACCINATION against tetanus but as the risk is small this is not usually considered necessary. However, if a dog receives a puncture wound, particularly if the injury occurs on farmland or where horses are grazing, a veterinary surgeon should be consulted and an anti-tetanus injection may be given.

thirst a dog should have access to clean drinking water at all times to satisfy its natural thirst and to replace water that has already been lost from the body. An increased thirst is usually a sign of illness or disorder and may be accompanied by other symptoms such as more or less urination, DIARRHOEA and VOMITING, fever, apathy and APPETITE LOSS. Causes include infections, kidney, thyroid gland and liver disorders, and DIABETES mellitus.

ticks *see* External parasites, page 77.

tongue worm *see* Parasites—Other internal parasites, page 70.

tourniquet *see* A–Z OF FIRST AID, bleeding, page 141.

tonsillitis inflammation of the tonsils—the small pink masses of lymphoid tissue situated on either side of the back of the mouth. The inflammation is caused by a bacterial or viral infection and results in swelling, redness, painful swallowing, fever, appetite loss and lethargy. The condition usually improves quite rapidly with antibiotics but it can be difficult to persuade the dog to eat and drink.

toxoplasmosis an infectious disease caused by a protozoan organism known as *Toxoplasma gondii*, which completes the sexual stage of its life cycle in cats. The organism passes out in the faeces of the cat as cysts that are then taken up by other mammals. These include rats and mice, farm animals, poultry, wild birds and dogs. All animals other than cats are intermediate hosts of the parasite. Once ingested, the parasites are carried by the bloodstream to other tissues and organs. Here they may either proliferate rapidly by asexual reproduction, causing an acute attack of the symptoms of toxoplasmosis, or they form cysts in tissues, which remain dormant. If the animal's immune system is compromised in any way or it becomes debilitated, the cysts may become active and replicate, once more causing an attack of symptoms. In general, the illness is mild but it can have serious consequences if contracted by a pregnant mammal. If toxoplasmosis is passed to unborn foetuses, it can produce deformities, brain damage, blindness and stillbirth.

Dogs are not usually infected by direct contact with cat faeces but by eating the raw flesh of other infected animals. People are infected by eating uncooked meat or through direct contact with cats with toxoplasma and are especially at risk when handling litter trays. However, dogs are not regarded as a means of human infection.

tracheal collapse a flattening of the windpipe or trachea, which can arise in older dogs of the toy breeds. The symptoms are noisy breathing and coughing, especially with exercise or when the dog becomes excited.

tracheal worm *see* PARASITES—Other internal parasites, page 70.

trench mouth a bacterial disease that can occur in dogs and is similar to trench fever, which was common among soldiers during the World War I. It usually arises in malnourished dogs or ones that are already ill from another cause. The infection causes a painful inflamed mouth and gums, with foul breath and possibly ulceration. Rarely, the lungs may become infected. Treatment involves use of antibiotics, and other drugs may also be needed. The dog may require special feeding and supplements of vitamins and minerals.

tumour any abnormal swelling that occurs in any part of the body, consists of an unusual growth of tissue and may be malignant or benign. Tumours tend to be classified according to the tissue of which they are composed, e.g. fibroma (mainly fibrous tissue) and myoma (largely muscle fibres). *See also* CANCER.

tunnel vision a disorder of vision in which an object is seen only if it is immediately in front of the eyes. This may occur in dogs with PROGRESSIVE RETINAL ATROPHY.

ulcer a break on the skin surface or on a mucous membrane lining a body cavity that is inflamed and often infected, failing to heal. Dogs can develop ulcers as a result of a variety of diseases and conditions. Sites include the mouth, skin and eyes.

uraemia the condition in which there is excess urea (the metabolic by-product of protein digestion) in the blood because of kidney disease or failure. A dog with this condition is extremely ill and often its chances of survival are slim.

urethra the duct carrying urine from the bladder out of the body, which is much shorter in bitches than in male dogs, making them more prone to CYSTITIS.

urethritis inflammation of the urethra, which in dogs is usually associated with CYSTITIS or BLADDER STONES. A dog that is obviously in pain when urinating and produces blood in the urine or a discharge should receive prompt veterinary treatment and normally requires antibiotic drugs.

vaccination the production of immunity to a disease by inoculation with a vaccine or a specially prepared material that stimulates the production of antibodies. (*See* ROUTINE CARE OF A DOG—Vaccination, page 41).

vomeronasal organs (Jacobson's organs) a pair of small olfactory organs, located near the roof of a dog's mouth, that contain cells sensitive to chemical odours. These organs form part of the mechanism that gives a dog its keen sense of smell.

vomiting (emesis) the reflex action whereby the stomach contents are expelled through the mouth because of the contraction of the diaphragm and abdominal wall muscles. Vomiting is caused by stimulus of the appropriate centre in the brain, but the primary agent is usually a sensation from the stomach itself, such as an irritant or toxic substance or gastric disease. Motion, travel or CAR SICKNESS is a further cause because of disturbance of the organs of balance in the inner ear.

The most usual cause of vomiting is simply a digestive upset because the dog has eaten something inappropriate or has gorged itself. If this is the case, there probably will not be any other symptoms. Food should not be given for twelve hours but a small quantity of water can be allowed after about two hours. If this does not provoke further vomiting, more water can be offered after about half an hour. If vomiting is persistent or accompanied by other symptoms such as obvious pain, DIARRHOEA, apathy, inability to urinate or passage of blood, then the dog should receive immediate veterinary examination to diagnose and treat the cause.

wart a solid, benign growth in the skin caused by a virus. Warts are usually best left alone but if they occur in an accessible spot, a dog will often bite or scratch them, causing bleeding. In this case, it is better to have them surgically removed.

wasp stings *see* BEE AND WASP STINGS.

weight loss unexplained weight loss in a dog is a cause for concern and evidence of some underlying disease or disorder that should always be investigated. The weight loss may not necessarily be accompanied by a lack of appetite, depending upon the underlying cause.

weil's disease *see* LEPTOSPIROSIS.

whipworm *see* PARASITES—Other internal parasites, page 70.

wobbler syndrome *see* PARALYSIS.

wounds *see* A–Z OF FIRST AID, page 150.

A-Z OF FIRST AID FOR DOGS

The aim of first aid, in dogs as in people, is to provide effective, on-the-spot treatment for an injury, illness or disorder when this is appropriate. The circumstances in which first aid is appropriate are:

1 when, without intervention, the dog would experience greater suffering,

2 its condition would further deteriorate,

3 it might die without immediate help.

In practice, it is not always obvious when these circumstances apply, and it can be difficult for an inexperienced person to know what to do. It is best, therefore, to make an immediate assessment, provide treatment when it is judged to be needed and telephone and/or transport the dog to a veterinary surgeon. First aid treatment may vary between something as simple as keeping the dog still, warm and calm, to giving artificial respiration. The following applies to simple measures that can be carried out by an inexperienced person, often in an emergency. In this context, it is important to stress that a person should attempt first aid only if it is safe to do so without risk of personal injury. It is often best to muzzle a dog, and this can be successfully done using a length of bandage or tape (*see* diagram on page 62, BEHAVIOURAL PROBLEMS IN DOGS—aggression).

artificial respiration artificial respiration is needed whenever a dog has stopped breathing, and it may also be the case that the heart has ceased to beat. The heart's action pumps blood around the body, and the brain soon suffers irrevocable damage if it is deprived of oxygen for more than a few minutes. Hence artificial respiration may be combined with heart massage in a technique known as CARDIOPULMONARY RESUSCITATION (CPR). There are a number of circumstances that may cause breathing to cease, including ANAPHYLACTIC SHOCK, ASPHYXIA, DROWNING, ELECTRIC SHOCK, accidental injuries, HAEMORRHAGE, CHOKING, SHOCK and concussion. If breathing is very shallow and slight, it can be difficult to detect. One way of checking is to hold a piece of tissue in front of the dog's nose, which will move when the animal breathes out. If breathing cannot be detected, action must be taken immediately to save the dog's life. The dog should be placed on its side with its head and neck extended forwards. The mouth and throat should be checked for any obstructions, with the tongue pulled forwards. Ideally, the dog's head should be lower than its body and the collar should be removed. Both hands should be placed over the ribs in the region of the chest and firm downward pressure should be exerted then immediately released. The downward pressure drives air out of the lungs, and these then expand and fill once more as the chest wall rises. The process should be repeated every twenty-five seconds with checks carried out to see if breathing has started. As

long as the heartbeat continues, artificial respiration will ensure
that vital oxygen is released into the blood. However, this technique is not effective if the dog has a punctured lung or a deep
wound or other injury to the chest cavity. If this is the case, it is
necessary to attempt the MOUTH-TO-NOSE method of artificial respiration in order to ventilate the lungs.

bleeding or **haemorrhage** bleeding may be either external, with
blood lost from a wound, or internal, in which organs or tissues
bleed inside the body. External bleeding is dangerous only if a
large blood vessel is involved, particularly if this is an artery, when
the amount lost is considerable and can quickly become life-threatening. If bleeding is from a smaller vessel, the blood normally clots
and seals off the cut end before too much harm is done. In the case
of profuse bleeding from an artery or a vein, an attempt must be
made to stop the flow by applying a pressure bandage. This is a
thick pad of any suitable absorbent material, ideally the sterile non-
stick dressings that can be purchased from pharmacists. In an emergency, however, any clean material can be used, such as a towel,
tea towel or sanitary towel. Pressure should be applied to the pad
for two minutes, and if it becomes soaked, another should be
placed on top. The whole should then be secured with a gauze or
crepe bandage so that it is firm but not too tight. The pressure exerted must be great enough to encourage clotting and the cessation
of bleeding, but not so tight as to cut off the blood circulation to
other tissues.

If it is clear that the pressure bandage is not working, then direct
pressure on the artery supplying the wound can be attempted to
stem the flow. The main pressure points are illustrated in the diagram on page 142. If serious arterial bleeding is occurring from a
wound in the limb, and this has not stopped with a pressure bandage, a tourniquet can be applied. A handkerchief, tie or strip of material is wrapped and tied tightly above the point of bleeding (nearest the body) and, if necessary, a pencil or other suitable instrument
is slipped between the layers and rotated to exert greater pressure.
In general, a tourniquet must be used very cautiously and never left
in place for more than ten minutes. Both this and direct pressure on
a pressure point should only be used as a last resort.

How to control severe external haemorrhage

Place the dog in an appropriate position and apply a thick pad of absorbent material to the wound.

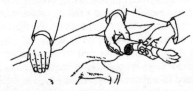

Firmly bandage the pad in place with a crêpe bandage, or a scarf or soft belt if a crêpe bandage is not available. If the pad becomes soaked through, then apply another pad and bandage it in place.

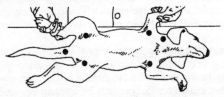

To temporarily control severe bleeding from the tail, foreleg, hindleg and head, press with the fingers at the appropriate points, as indicated.

A dog's ears are very liable to injury and tend to bleed profusely. If the flap of the ear is bleeding, a clean, absorbent pad should be placed on either side and pressure applied with the fingers for some minutes. With the pads still in place, the injured ear should be laid flat across the head and secured firmly with a crepe bandage, if one is available. This should be wrapped around the head and throat several times, taking care not to tighten it up too much as this may restrict the dog's breathing. The uninjured ear should be left free and this helps to prevent the bandage from slipping. If bleeding is coming from within the ear, the opening should be plugged with a suitably sized clean pad before bandaging.

If bleeding is from a wound on the tongue or any part of the mouth, it is difficult to apply direct pressure with a conscious dog because of the risk of being bitten. The head should be kept low so that blood flows downwards and outwards to minimize the risk of choking. Depending on the site of the wound, it may be possible to pinch the skin externally and apply pressure in that way.

If blood is coming from the nose, no attempt should be made to cover the nostrils as again there is a risk of choking. A pad soaked in cold water and then wrung out should be placed over the bridge of the nose in an attempt to stop the bleeding. It may be the case, however, that the bleeding is caused by some internal injury, in which case this measure is not likely to help. Bleeding from the eye should be treated in a similar way. A clean pad, soaked in cold water and then wrung out, should be gently held over the eye while the dog is being restrained.

It is not uncommon for a dog to cut or break a claw and this may bleed profusely. The wound should be covered with a clean dressing and the paw bandaged. No attempt should be made to remove the broken claw and the dog should be taken to a veterinary surgeon.

Internal bleeding usually results from a severe blow to the body or head. It most commonly occurs as a result of a road traffic accident but may be the result of a fall from a height onto a hard surface. A further hazard for farm dogs is being kicked or trodden on by larger animals. Internal bleeding is very serious, as unless it quickly stops the dog is likely to go into shock. In some cases, there may be some issue of blood from the mouth, nose and ears or it may be present in vomit, urine or faeces. The dog should be laid on its side with its head and neck extended, and a pillow or folded coat, etc, placed under the rear quarters and hind legs. The dog should be covered with a blanket and taken to a veterinary clinic without delay.

bloat bloat is a condition that can affect large, deep-chested dogs such as Great Danes although it may occur in smaller breeds as well. The dog's stomach becomes bloated with gas and expands to such an extent that it interferes with respiration. Rolling around on the ground after eating a meal or other sudden exercise are predisposing factors, as are eating or drinking too much. Early signs of bloat include a swollen abdomen and severe pain, breathing difficulties, retching, agitation and increased salivation. The main risk is the development of SHOCK, which can occur quite rapidly. A dog showing any of these symptoms should be taken immediately to a veterinary clinic for emergency treatment.

broken bones and **dislocations** (*see also* DISLOCATION and FRACTURE in A–Z OF ILLNESSES, INJURIES AND VETERINARY PROCEDURES, pages 97 and 105) dogs can sustain broken or dislocated bones as a result of falls, catching or trapping a limb, being kicked by a farm animal or other trauma. One of the most common causes, however, is road traffic accidents. These injuries are extremely painful, and it is usually necessary to muzzle a dog before attempting to deal with them.

limbs the dog should be persuaded to lie in its bed or basket with the injured limb uppermost. A clean folded towel should be gently pulled beneath the injured leg to provide some support. If a broken bone is protruding through the skin (open fracture), this should be covered with another clean towel or pad of suitable material.

back spinal fractures are potentially very serious and may result in paralysis of the area of the body below the injury. The dog should be gently slid onto a firm surface, such as a large flat piece of wood or folding picnic table, which can be used as a rigid stretcher. However, in lifting the dog, great care must be taken not to move the spine as this may cause further damage. Ideally, two people should move the dog, supporting the whole length of the back.

ribs if fractured or dislocated ribs are suspected, a length of bandage or other suitable, clean material can be wrapped around the dog's back and chest to provide support. Care should be taken not to bandage too tightly. If the dog is having any difficulty in breathing, it may be suspected that a broken rib has punctured a lung. Obviously, in this case the dog should not be muzzled and should be persuaded to lie in its bed.

tail a dog's tail is susceptible to fracture through being caught, crushed or even run over by the wheel of a vehicle. The tail may hang limply at an odd angle or appear to be swollen. It is difficult to bandage a tail successfully and, provided that there is no bleeding, this is not necessary as long as the dog is taken for veterinary examination and treatment.

In all cases of suspected fracture or dislocation, the dog should be taken immediately to a veterinary surgeon. It should not be offered anything to eat or drink as it is likely to be given a general anaesthetic so that the injury can be dealt with.

burns and scalds burns and scalds produce similar symptoms, but the former are caused by dry heat and the latter by moist heat. Burns may also be caused by electric currents and caustic chemicals. Like small children, dogs are at risk of burns and scalds in the home, and it is wise to take sensible precautions. It is not unusual, for instance, for a dog to be scalded through upsetting a drink of hot tea or coffee over itself or from knocking over a kettle or pan. Burns to the nose and mouth are quite common when the dog samples very hot food, and barbecues present a particular risk.

Another common type of injury is scorching or burning by lying too close to a fire. A dog should always be kept away when caustic chemicals are being used in the home (e.g. paint stripper, oven cleaner, etc), and these must be stored safely out of reach. A puppy or young dog still at the chewing stage is at risk of electric shock or burns by biting flexes. It should not be allowed near electric appliances, and these must be switched off and unplugged if the dog has to be left alone. Obviously, if a dog is in contact with a live electricity supply, the first priority is to disconnect this safely before attending to the patient (*see* ELECTRIC SHOCK).

Formerly burns were classified by 'degrees' but they are now described either as 'superficial', where sufficient tissue remains to ensure regrowth, or 'deep'. With deep burns, all the affected layers of skin are destroyed and underlying tissues are exposed. Healing is prolonged and difficult, and there is usually considerable scarring, pain and disfigurement. With all burns, but particularly with deep ones, the main risk is the development of shock and infection. Sometimes, especially in dogs with abundant fur, the extent of the damage is not immediately apparent, and blisters and weeping wounds may appear some time later. First aid treatment consists of soaking the area with cold water for about ten or fifteen minutes. Cold water can be poured over the burn or a shower attachment may be used. If the skin is intact, a clean, non-stick dressing and bandage can be placed over the area and a veterinary surgeon should be contacted for further advice. If the skin is broken, the wound should ideally be covered with a clean, sterile, non-stick medical dressing, which is bandaged into place. However, in an emergency any clean covering may be used, such as a tea towel or pillow case, and the dog must be taken immediately to a veterinary clinic. If burns are either deep or extensive, the outlook is usually poor, and a veterinary surgeon may advise euthanasia to avoid further suffering.

cardiopulmonary resuscitation (CPR) an emergency procedure combining MOUTH-TO-NOSE RESUSCITATION with heart massage. It is used as a last resort to try to save the life of a dog that has ceased to breathe and has no heartbeat. The dog should be laid on its side, its mouth opened, tongue pulled forward and any visible debris removed. The tongue should then be pushed back and the mouth gently closed. With the dog's head and neck extended forward, place one hand around the muzzle. Then place the mouth completely over the dog's nose and blow into the nostrils so that the lungs are inflated. The mouth should then be removed, allowing the rib cage to fall and the lungs to deflate before the procedure is repeated. Mouth-to-nose resuscitation should continue for about ten seconds followed by heart massage, if the heartbeat is still absent. If the dog is small, place one hand at its back and the other around its rib cage and press forward firmly while compressing the ribs together. This should be repeated quickly at a rate of about 120 squeezes per minute. With a larger dog, the hands are placed palms downwards and one on top of the other on the rib cage just behind the front leg. Pressure is exerted firmly downwards and forwards and the action should be repeated at a rate of about 100 times per minute. With a very large, deep-chested dog, it is better to roll the animal onto its back and apply strong, vigorous downward pressure in the same way, on the breastbone where it joins the rib cage. Considerable strength is needed and the downward pressure should be exerted for a count of two and released for a count of one. This should be carried out at a rate of 80 compressions per minute.

Whatever the method used, heart massage should be carried out for fifteen seconds and then a check made to see if the pulse has returned. (To check for a heartbeat, the fingers should be placed on the left-hand side of the chest immediately behind the front leg.) Mouth-to-nose resuscitation must then be repeated if the dog is not breathing. An alternative method, if there are two people, is for one to carry out heart massage for five seconds followed by the second person giving one breath into the dog's lungs. Frequent checks should be made for the return of heartbeat and breathing. As long as the heart is beating, mouth-to-nose resuscitation will provide the dog with sufficient oxygen to maintain life. It should be given for three seconds, allowing the lungs to deflate fully after each breath, followed by a pause of two seconds to see if the dog starts to breathe on its own.

choking violent coughing and inability to breathe because of obstruction of the windpipe by an object that the dog has picked up in its mouth. This object may be a food item, ball or other toy, pebble, etc. Choking is very frightening and distressing, both for the dog and anyone watching. Action must be taken immediately to save the dog's life but with sensible precautions to lessen the risk of being bitten. While it remains conscious, a choking dog is extremely frightened, agitated and fighting for breath. Ideally, one person should restrain the dog and, depending on size, the easiest way of achieving this may be to grasp the body between the legs. Wearing strong gloves, the person should open the dog's mouth by grasping the upper and lower jaw in either hand, pressing the lips and gums over the teeth. A second person can then reach inside the mouth and attempt to dislodge the trapped object, either using the fingers or a suitable instrument to hook it forwards. It is obviously easier to attempt this if the dog has lost consciousness, but in both instances it is essential to work quickly and there is a risk of pushing the object farther down.

If, as is sometimes the case, the object can be clearly seen to be stuck in the mouth and lodged between the teeth, there is little alternative but to attempt to remove it in this way. If it has dropped farther down and is blocking the entrance to the windpipe at the back of the throat, other methods can be tried. If the dog is a large one, HEIMLICH'S MANOEUVRE can be attempted. The dog is lifted onto its hind legs by a person standing behind, with the arms encircling the chest. A fist is made with one hand placed just below the ribs. Using the free hand, the fist is thrust firmly into the body with a rapid forward and upward push, which may need to be repeated several times. As a result of this, the object is propelled outwards into the dog's mouth. Alternatively, if the dog is not conscious, it can be laid on its side and the hands placed one on top of the other over the ribs, as for ARTIFICIAL RESPIRATION. The rib cage is then pressed firmly and rapidly downwards, which expels a burst of air from the lungs and with luck dislodges the object blocking the windpipe. A small, unconscious dog can be held round the top of the hind legs, turned upside down, swung from side to side and lightly shaken to dislodge the object. If this does not work, the dog should be laid down with one hand placed on its back and the other on its abdomen just below the rib cage. The lower hand squeezes rapidly forwards and upwards to cause a sudden rush of air from the lungs in a variation of Heimlich's manoeuvre.

With all these procedures it is necessary to ensure that the dislodged object is removed from the dog's mouth. Once the airway is clear the dog may or may not begin to breathe spontaneously, hence it may be necessary to administer artificial respiration, MOUTH-TO-NOSE RESUSCITATION or CARDIOPULMONARY RESUSCITATION, depending on the circumstances. In all cases, the dog should be taken for immediate veterinary examination as its throat may have sustained injuries that require treatment and to ensure that its condition is stable.

convulsions or **fits** *see* A–Z OF ILLNESSES, INJURIES AND VETERINARY PROCEDURES, page 91.

drowning many dogs love water and swimming, but they are unable to anticipate risk or danger and so it is not unusual for them to get into difficulties. It is also the case that all too often a person drowns while attempting to rescue a dog. Although it may be very distressing, therefore, never enter unknown and potentially danger-

ous water in an attempt to rescue a dog. If possible, the dog should
be hooked by a pole from the bank or thrown something that it may
be able to climb on to to pull itself clear of the water.

If the dog has started to drown, its lungs will be filled with water.
A small dog should be held upside down by the hips and swung and
shaken to drain out water. A large dog should be similarly turned
upside down by being held around its middle. The dog may or may
not begin to cough and splutter as a result. It should be laid on its
side with the head lower than the body and a check made for
breathing and heartbeat. If the heart is beating but breathing is absent, either ARTIFICIAL RESPIRATION or MOUTH-TO-NOSE RESUSCITATION
should be given. If neither heartbeat nor respiration is present then
CARDIOPULMONARY RESUSCITATION should be tried. Even if the dog
apparently recovers, there is a possible risk of complications, particularly SHOCK, developing at a later stage.

electric shock dogs suffer electric shock by chewing the cables of
household appliances, and young animals and puppies are usually
most at risk. More rarely, a dog may wander on to a live electric
railway line or be struck by lightning. Of course, in many cases the
electric shock is instantly fatal or there may be severe burns. The
first priority is to isolate the dog safely from the power source. Unless this can be safely accomplished, no attempt should be made to
move the animal. Once this has been achieved, a check should be
made for heartbeat and respiration and if these are absent, CARDIO-
PULMONARY RESUSCITATION should be carried out. If this is successful, the dog should be taken immediately to a veterinary surgery for
further treatment and monitoring. There is a possible risk of complications, especially shock, developing after electrocution.

Heimlich's manoeuvre *see* CHOKING.

mouth-to-nose resuscitation a type of artificial respiration that
may be given to a dog that has ceased to breathe. It involves holding the dog's mouth shut with a hand around the muzzle. The dog's
nose is then covered with the mouth and air blown directly into the
nostrils to inflate the lungs. The chest expands as this occurs and
then the mouth is removed so that the lungs can deflate. The process is repeated and continued until the dog begins to breathe spontaneously, and checks should be made for the return of breathing at

regular intervals. This method of artificial respiration is the best
one to use if the dog has any form of deep chest wound or there is
reason to suspect that there may be lung damage. Frothy blood, i.e.
mixed with air, coming from the nose or mouth or appearing at the
wound surface is one indication of such damage.

shock physiological shock is a condition of acute circulatory failure in which the arterial blood pressure is too low to provide the
normal blood and oxygen supply to the body. In dogs, shock can
arise following any illness, injury, accident or trauma. It can occur
quite soon after a particular incident or arise much later following
an apparent recovery. It is a serious and potentially life-threatening
and must be dealt with immediately should any signs occur.

One important early indication of shock is pallor of the gums.
These should normally be definitely pink, and if a portion is
pinched between a finger and thumb, the blood, and hence colour,
should return immediately. In early shock, the colour is very pale
and is slow in returning when the gum is pinched. Other indications
include rapid breathing and heartbeat rate, restlessness or apathy.
Later the breathing becomes slow and slight and the heartbeat is irregular, the dog slips into unconsciousness and has white or blue-
tinged gums and a lowered body temperature of 36.7°C or less.
First aid treatment consists of lying the dog down on its side and
stretching the head and neck forwards. Cushions, folded blankets
or whatever is available should be used to raise the hindquarters so
that blood flows forwards. ARTIFICIAL RESPIRATION, heart massage or
CARDIOPULMONARY RESUSCITATION may be needed, and the dog
should be covered with a blanket to keep it warm. Immediate,
emergency veterinary treatment is needed, and the dog is likely to
require close monitoring and intensive care.

wounds the severity of a wound varies from serious and life-
threatening to relatively minor. All carry the risk of infection and
need, therefore, to be thoroughly cleaned. If there is profuse bleeding, this should be dealt with first. A minor wound can be thoroughly washed with plenty of warm water containing an antiseptic
solution, and a clean dressing and bandage can then be applied. If a
wound is obviously deep or severe, however, it is best not to waste
time trying to deal with it at home but to cover it with clean mate-

rial and get immediate veterinary assistance (*see* BLEEDING). Any wound, including one with stitches following an operation, can become infected. Signs of infection include heat, swelling, pain and a discharge containing pus. If this occurs, the dog should be taken to a veterinary surgeon for treatment. It will probably require antibiotic drugs and may need sedation or general anaesthetic so that the wound can be thoroughly cleaned and dressed.

A-Z OF BREEDS OF DOGS

For information on the conditions mentioned in the following entries refer to the individual entries that appear in the A–Z OF ILL-NESSES, INJURIES AND VETERINARY PROCEDURES, which begins on page 79.

affenpinscher or **monkey terrier** one of the less common toy breeds with a black, shaggy, wiry coat and an average height at the shoulder of 24–28 cm (9–11 ins). It is a tough little character, game for anything, and makes a good family pet.

Afghan hound a strikingly attractive, tall, slim dog with long, silky fur. It is a light tan colour on the head and body and creamy white on the limbs, with a narrow black muzzle and long, dangling ears. The dog stands about 68–74 cm (27–29 ins) at the shoulder and, while it is an affectionate pet, it can be quite excitable and may be disobedient. Afghan hounds were bred for hunting and have excellent keen sight. If infected with infectious canine hepatitis, they may have a tendency to develop the eye opacity known as 'blue eye'. The coat of the Afghan needs a great deal of care, attention and grooming to keep the dog looking its best. It is most suitable for experienced dog owners with plenty of free time.

akita: Japanese akita an uncommon breed with a long history that stretches back for thousands of years. It is a large dog with pricked ears, mainly black in colour but with some white, especially on the underside and legs. The average height is in the order of 66–71 cm (26–28 ins) at the shoulder, and it is a strong, energetic dog needing plenty to do. It is generally obedient with its owners but is not always tolerant of other dogs.

Alaskan malamute an uncommon breed of dog that is large and powerful with an abundance of long fur. It was bred to work as a member of a team pulling a sled across the ice and snow and can have a dominant and independent nature although it is loyal and loving to its owners. It is given to howling and prone to an inherited defect that causes haemolytic anaemia. It is a breed more suited to a specialist dog owner with plenty of time to devote to its needs.

basenji (Congo dog) an attractive, medium-sized tan and white dog that originally came from Central Africa. It is an uncommon breed showing several unusual features, with pricked ears and a tail curled over its back. The basenji is short-haired and stands about 43 cm (17 ins) high at the shoulder. European specimens are descended from about twelve original members of the breed. It is unusual in that a particular arrangement of the vocal cords makes it unable to bark, although it is capable of making a peculiar yodelling sound. Also, bitches of the breed come into season only once in the year, generally in the autumn, compared to a more normal twice-yearly heat period. European basenjis are liable to a number of inherited disorders, including haemolytic anaemia, kidney and eye problems, that have probably arisen through inbreeding. They have some cat-like characteristics in that they are adept climbers and use their front paws to wash the face. They were bred for hunting and have a definite mind of their own, although they are loving towards their owners. They tend to be 'one-person' dogs, and become strongly bonded to their owner and may pine if separated.

basset: Fauve de Bretagne an uncommon small breed that comes from Brittany in France. It stands about 32–38 cm (12–15 ins) at the shoulder and is tan-coloured with a wiry coat and pendulous ears. It was bred for hunting and is a tough and energetic little dog that is game for anything. It is affectionate and friendly and makes a good family pet.

basset: petit basset griffon vendéen a small breed of French hunting dog that reaches a height of 34–38 cm (13–15 ins) at the shoulder and somewhat resembles a SPANIEL. It has a long shaggy coat and is tan and cream in colour with pendulous ears. It is a game little dog that is ready for anything and needs plenty of exercise.

basset hound a small, solid dog that has surprisingly short legs and is black, tan and white in colour, reaching a height of about 33–36 cm (13–14 ins). It has long, pendulous ears and a particularly keen sense of smell. It is prone to the development of bladder stones, which may cause urinary incontinence. The basset hound makes a loveable family pet and is usually good-natured and friendly. Care should be taken with feeding to ensure that it does not become too fat and exercise should be encouraged. It was originally bred to hunt hares.

beagle a small breed of hound having the colours black, white and tan and reaching a height of 33 cm (13 ins) at the shoulder. It was bred as a hunter of hares and has a friendly, loveable nature, making it a good family pet. Beagles have a tendency to gain weight so care should be taken with feeding and they should be encouraged to have plenty of exercise. They may occasionally suffer from an inherited enzyme deficiency that causes haemolytic anaemia, but they rarely suffer from any form of tumour.

Bernese mountain dog a large, handsome breed with an abundant long coat that is mostly black but with a white chest and some tan on the face, chest and legs. Its height at the shoulder is in the order of 64–70 cm (25–27 ins), and it is a strong, faithful and obedient dog that responds well to training. The Bernese can make a loveable family pet but needs plenty of house room because of its large size.

Bichon Frise this little dog has a fluffy, curly white coat that requires a great deal of grooming. It reaches a height of only 23–28 cm (9–11 ins) at the shoulder and is a charming and intelligent, loveable family dog. Although only small, it is game for anything and more than willing to join in with whatever is going on.

bloodhound a large, solid-looking hound, standing about 66 cm (26 ins) at the shoulder with an appearance that makes it instantly recognizable. The bloodhound is black and tan in colour with folds of loose skin and eyes that sometimes appear bloodshot, all of which give it a rather mournful expression. It is renowned for its ability to follow a scent and is used by police forces for tracking. The bloodhound is generally friendly and good-natured but can be shy and nervous with strangers. The breed has a tendency to develop the eye disorder known as ectropion in which the eyelids curve outwards, and its sight may be impaired by the highly folded skin on the face.

borzoi a striking, tall, thin breed of dog with a beautiful long, wavy, silky coat that is usually white and tan in colour. This aristocratic-looking dog reaches a height of about 74 cm (29 ins) at the shoulder and somewhat resembles a long-haired greyhound. The borzoi was bred in Russia for hunting wolves and is very fleet of foot, being able to run for many miles without tiring. Because of this, it may not return very readily when called and requires an experienced owner with plenty of time to devote to its exercise and grooming.

bouvier des Flandres a large, sturdy dog bred in the Netherlands and Belgium and used for herding farm animals. It reaches a height of about 62–68 cm (25–26 ins) at the shoulder and has a shaggy, rough, wavy coat, grey in colour. The bouvier is tough and adaptable and makes a good family pet as it is intelligent and easy to train. Some members of the breed have a tendency to inherit a defect of the larynx, resulting in breathing difficulties and affecting the ability to bark.

boxer with its squashed, square, wrinkled face and alert, friendly expression, the boxer is instantly recognizable and a great favourite with many people, especially children. The boxer is a large, strong, sturdy dog reaching a height of about 57–63 cm (22–25 ins) at the shoulder. The coat is very short, and colours vary from brindled to white and tan. The boxer is extremely good-natured, full of fun and ready for anything, needing plenty of exercise and good, firm training. It makes a loveable family dog but, like many of the flat-faced (brachycephalic) breeds, is relatively short-lived, not usually surviving beyond ten. It is subject to breathing problems and is susceptible to heatstroke because of this. There is a marked susceptibility towards the formation of tumours, which may be cancerous.

Boxers have a tendency towards the development of Cushing's syndrome (a hormonal disorder) and are susceptible to tearing the ligament of the stifle joint of the hind leg, which can lead to osteoarthritis.

briard a large, shaggy-coated breed that may originally have come from the Brie region of France. It bears a passing resemblance to the OLD ENGLISH SHEEPDOG, with its abundance of long fur that covers its eyes, and is unusual in having double dew claws on the hind limbs. The colours are different, however, being a mixture of tan and black, although the briard was similarly bred for herding farm animals. It is an intelligent and easy-going dog, reaching a height of 62–68 cm (24–28 ins) at the shoulder, and can make a good family pet. It needs a dedicated owner, however, with plenty of time to spend on grooming, and also requires plenty of exercise.

Brittany as the name suggests, this medium-sized breed of gundog has its origins in the Brittany region of France. This intelligent, long-coated dog was bred for hunting, pointing and retrieving and is usually white and tan in colour. It reaches a height of about 51 cm (20 ins) at the shoulder and makes a good-natured household pet as well as a useful gundog.

buhund or **Norwegian buhund** a medium-sized, rough-coated dog with a height at the shoulder of about 45 cm (18 ins) that slightly resembles a small husky. The colours are a mixture of fawn, white and black, and the tail is held curved over the back. This is an energetic and game little dog that thrives on exercise and can make a loyal family pet and good watchdog.

bulldog: English bulldog with its large, square head and squashed, flattened face, the English bulldog is another breed that is instantly recognizable. These small, stout, powerful dogs are short-haired and variable in colour but are often a mixture of white, tan and black. The bulldog became a national symbol of England for its characteristics of courage, loyalty and tenacity, but was bred for the cruel sport of bull-baiting. The large, broad head of the bulldog causes problems for bitches of this breed in delivering puppies. Also, the squashed face makes breathing difficult, and they are prone to respiratory problems and are relatively short-lived, with an average life expectancy of seven to eight years. The bulldog makes a loveable if noisy family pet (as it tends to snort, snore and slobber) and needs little exercise or grooming.

bulldog: French bulldog much smaller than its English counterpart, the French bulldog has a friendly and placid nature and makes an ideal family pet. It is usually dark or brindled in colour with some white, and has pricked ears and short hair that requires little in the way of grooming. It has the broad head and squashed face typical of these breeds and has a tendency to suffer from breathing problems.

bull mastiff a large, broad and powerful breed, reaching a height at the shoulder of 64–69 cm (25–27 ins), which can be a formidable guard dog. It is believed to have been derived from crossing ENGLISH BULLDOGS with English mastiffs, and usually has a dark brown, brindled coat with some black coloration. It has a short broad face, but less extreme than that of the bulldog or boxer, and is energetic and intelligent, requiring plenty of exercise and good training. This breed is probably more suitable for an experienced owner with plenty of time to devote to its needs.

Caanan dog an uncommon breed believed to have an ancient ancestry in the the Middle East. It has a light golden coat of medium length with some white, pricked pointed ears and a keen, intelligent appearance. It is rewarding to train and makes a loyal family pet and excellent guard dog. It is of medium to large size, reaching a height at the shoulder of 51–61 cm (20–24 ins).

cattle dog or **Australian cattle dog** a medium-sized working dog bred in Australia for work on cattle ranches. It reaches a height of 46–51 cm (18–20 ins) at the shoulder and has a dark grey, brindled coat mixed with tan. Its fur is of medium length, and it has pricked ears and an alert, intelligent appearance. It is an uncommon breed in Europe but is a hardy and loyal family dog as well as an excellent working animal.

Chihuahua named after a region in Mexico, the Chihuahua is the smallest of all the toy breeds and can easily be held tucked under one arm. It is a lively, intelligent little dog that makes a lot of noise for one of such small size. It tends to yap frequently and often is not friendly towards children or strangers. Chihuahuas may be short or long-haired and exhibit a variety of colours. They are ideal pets for those with limited space and do not need long walks.

Chihuahua bitches may experience difficulties in giving birth because of the relatively large size of their puppies' heads. This dome-shaped head is also associated with an increased risk of hydrocephalus.

Chin: Japanese Chin an attractive toy breed with an abundance of very long, silky hair with black, white and grey coloration. It has a short, squashed face, long ears and plumed tail, and very much resembles the PEKINESE. It is bright and lively and makes an ideal dog for those with a limited amount of space. Also, it does not require a great deal of exercise but, like several of the toy breeds, it can be intolerant of children. The coat of the Japanese Chin requires a great deal of grooming to keep it in good order, but it is a rewarding and affectionate pet.

chow-chow a sturdy, medium-sized breed of dog that came originally from China and has the unique feature of possessing a bluish-black tongue and gums because of the presence of the pigment melanin. Although not very common, chows are one of the breeds that are instantly recognizable, and they reach a height of 53–56 cm (21–22 ins) at the shoulder. They have a broad head and small, pricked ears and an exceptionally thick coat of dense, reddish-bronze fur tinged here and there with a lighter shade. Even in the British climate, a chow can become extremely uncomfortable in hot weather and has a reputation for being bad-tempered and snappy, especially towards children. Chows need firm handling and good training as they can be stubborn but are good guard dogs. In addition to their unusual mouth, another uncommon feature is that they do not become tied together during mating. Chows tend to have small eyes for the size of their head and are prone to a condition of the eyelids called entropion. Some individuals suffer from an inherited condition called hereditary myotonia, in which the muscles are subject to a phase of spasm and twitching, especially after an extended period of rest.

collie: bearded collie the bearded collie is an attractive dog of medium size, reaching a height of 53–56 cm (21 to 22 ins) at the shoulder. It has an abundant coat of long, silky grey and white hair that needs a considerable amount of grooming to keep it tidy. It is an active and intelligent dog that responds well to training but needs to be kept occupied with plenty of exercise. The bearded collie can be an ideal dog for an active, country-living family and is good-natured and always ready to join in.

collie: Border collie the familiar black and white working collie, which is a common dog on farms throughout the British Isles, especially those devoted to sheep-rearing. The Border collie is very intelligent and responds well to complex training, often building up an intuitive relationship with its handler, exhibiting a high degree of skill. This dog is happiest when it is working, often as part of a team, and is hardy with a great deal of endurance and stamina. Border collies are medium-sized dogs reaching a height of about 53 cm (21 ins) at the shoulder. Dogs from good working families are valuable animals that are much sought after and priced accordingly. They tend to retain a strong herding instinct and may try to round up other pets or children. For this reason, not all individuals make good family dogs unless their owners have sufficient time to give them plenty of exercise and attention. Border collies are prone to the eye disorder known as progressive retinal atrophy.

collie: rough collie an attractive and elegant long-haired collie, made famous in the television series *Lassie*. Rough collies reach a height of 56–61 cm (22–24 ins) at the shoulder and show various coat colours, usually mixtures of white, tan and black. They are good-natured and intelligent, responding well to training, and make good family pets although they need a great deal of grooming to keep the coat in order. Care is needed to balance feeding and exercise as rough collies are inclined to become obese.

collie: smooth collie this dog is the same in all respects as the rough collie except that it has been bred to have a smooth coat.

Chinese crested dog this highly unusual, comical-looking little dog comes both in a hairless and long-haired variety and reaches a height of 28–33 cm (11–13 ins) at the shoulder. The smooth variety has no hair on its body but has a silky, fluffy white plume on its head, ankles and tail. The long-haired variety shows similar colours of dark grey and white, and also has the same arrangement of plumes. In spite of its small size, it can be a good watchdog and makes an appealing, good-natured and intelligent pet.

corgi: Welsh Cardigan corgi a slightly larger corgi than the WELSH PEMBROKE, reaching a height of 30 cm (12 ins) at the shoulder, the usual colours being tan and white but with other variations. The Cardigan corgi is hardly, loyal and intelligent but is perhaps best suited to a home without children. Individuals have a tendency to develop degenerative eye disorders involving the retina. Corgis of both breeds are inclined to develop bladder stones.

corgi: Welsh Pembroke corgi this corgi is the breed that has become familiar as favourite pets of the British royal family. Pembroke corgis were bred for herding cattle, particularly for running in and nipping at the heels to keep the animals moving. Corgis have earned a reputation for being bad-tempered and snappy, but a great deal depends upon the individual dog's training and temperament. They are tough, loyal and game little dogs, which need to be active as they have a tendency to become obese. The usual height at the shoulder is between 25 and 30 cm (10 and 12 ins), and the most common colours are tan and white. They are probably best suited to a home without children and make loyal pets and good watchdogs. Corgis can be prone to back problems, particularly slipped discs.

dachshund a breed that is very familiar to most people, being popularly and affectionately known as 'the sausage dog'. Dachshunds occur in miniature and standard sizes but are all small, long-backed dogs on short legs. Also, they occur as smooth or short-haired, long-haired and wiry-coated varieties, and the usual colours are tan or tan and black. They were bred in Germany for hunting badgers, their small size making it possible for them to go down the setts. As a consequence, dachshunds are brave and intelligent and make loyal household pets and good watchdogs as they are inclined to bark a lot. Unfortunately, the long back makes the dachshund vulnerable to problems, especially a slipped disc. These problems are made worse by obesity, and great care must be taken to ensure that dachshunds do not become overweight. (Since their legs are so short an obese dog is likely to walk with its belly dragging along the ground.) Dachshunds are prone to some other disorders, particularly the development of bladder stones but also diabetes mellitus in middle age.

Dalmatian another very familiar and much loved breed, known affectionately as 'the spotty dog' and made even more popular by the Disney film *101 Dalmatians*. Dalmatians are white with black or dark brown spots and are large dogs, reaching a height of 58–61 cm (23–24 ins) at the shoulder. The breed was developed in England to follow after the carriages of the aristocracy. They are good-natured, bouncy, friendly dogs that require a great deal of exercise and plenty of space. In common with several other white breeds, Dalmatians are prone to deafness and are also inclined to develop bladder stones.

deerhound one of the largest breeds, reaching a height of 76 cm (30 ins) at the shoulder and similar to the IRISH WOLFHOUND. The deerhound is an ancient Scottish breed that was used for hunting wolves, wild boar and deer. It is lean, fast and athletic with a long, shaggy grey and fawn-coloured coat. The deerhound is brave, friendly and intelligent, and makes a loyal family dog. Because of its large size, however, it needs plenty of exercise, space and feeding and is now relatively uncommon.

Doberman (pinscher) a handsome, large and powerful breed with very short hair and predominantly black in colour but with highlights of tan on the face, legs and abdomen. The Doberman was originally bred in Germany in the 19th century and is used as a guard dog. It is named after a Dr Louis Doberman and is a muscular, powerful animal that can be formidable and aggressive if not well trained and controlled. Dobermans tend to have a dominant personality and do not make good family dogs, especially if there are children in the home.

elkhound a strong, sturdy breed, originating in Norway, which has a coat of dense fur in shades of grey and a highly curled tail held over the back. It is a medium-sized dog, reaching a height of about 52 cm (20 ins) at the shoulder, and was bred as a hunter. It is extremely hardy and able to withstand the coldest weather, although less happy when subjected to heat. The elkhound is intelligent and friendly, although it can have a wilful streak and so needs to be well trained. It requires plenty of exercise and careful feeding as it is inclined to become obese. Elkhounds have a tendency to suffer from a degenerative disorder of the retina, which affects their sight. They are fairly uncommon outside their native Norway.

foxhound a medium-sized hound bred in Britain to hunt in packs after foxes. Foxhounds are short-haired and the coat colour is variable but usually with large patches of black, tan and white. Foxhounds have a keen sense of smell and bay excitedly when on the trail of a fox. Traditionally they were bred for hunting rather than as household pets and are becoming much less common as fox-hunting has declined. Retired hounds do not make ideal family pets, and the fate of dogs too old or disabled for the hunt has been the cause of much controversy.

Great Dane a giant of a dog, reaching a height of at least 76 cm (30 ins) at the shoulder, which was originally bred in Germany. Great Danes are short-coated dogs and colours vary from mainly tan to a more variable appearance with stripes of darker brown. They were bred for hunting and were capable of tackling wolves and wild boar, being swift and courageous. Great Danes are lively, intelligent and playful, but because of their size this can be a prob-lem in an ordinary family home. However, they are good-natured and affectionate and can make good house dogs provided there is plenty of space available. Care should be taken not to over-exercise a Great Dane puppy before adulthood as this can lead to permanent joint disabilities. Also, they are prone to a disorder of the vertebrae in the neck, which causes squeezing of the spinal cord, affecting control of the limbs. The dog suffers from an intermittent, partial paralysis, causing it to stagger (known as 'wobbler syndrome). Some individuals that inherit a particular, variable coat colour (har-lequin) may be prone to deafness and blindness. It is believed that the gene responsible for the coat coloration is also linked to these disorders. Great Danes require a great deal of feeding and plenty of exercise, and are best suited to living in the countryside. Some in-dividuals are prone to digestive upsets, particularly diarrhoea.

greyhound another breed that is instantly recognizable, being a tall, thin dog that is very fleet of foot. A greyhound reaches a height of 71–76 cm (28–30 ins) at the shoulder and has a short coat show-ing a variety of colours from tan to dark brown or brindled. Like the cheetah among cats, the greyhound is built for speed and was bred for hunting, especially hare coursing. It hunts by sight rather than scent, and in recent times its athletic prowess has been much exploited in the sport of greyhound racing. Greyhounds show sev-eral unusual features, such as having a comparatively large heart and different blood cells. They have a comparatively high concen-tration of red blood cells. When kept in racing kennels, they have a tendency to be infected with the dog tapeworm *Dipylidium caninum* and the whipworm *Trichuris vulpis*, but this may reflect the fact that parasites spread more easily under these circumstances. (*See also* PARASITES—Internal parasites, pages 68–70)

Greyhounds have little or no body fat and this, coupled with their thin coat, makes them susceptible to cold. Hence it may be necessary to fit them with a coat in very cold weather. If brought up to be pets they can be good-natured and affectionate, but retired racing greyhounds can find it difficult to adjust to life in a home and patience is needed.

Italian greyhound essentially a miniature greyhound, it is classed as a toy breed and is an intelligent and lively little dog that makes an excellent family pet. It is a game little dog, requiring plenty of activity and exercise.

griffon bruxellois a small, sturdy breed that very much resembles a terrier and may have either a long or a short coat. It originates from Belgium, being named after the city of Brussels, and is a loveable and lively pet and good watchdog. The colour is a mixture of tan and brown, and the griffon has a short face and strong body and is always ready for action.

Hamiltonstovare a medium-sized attractive breed of hound with a short coat, coloured black, tan and white. This dog reaches a height of 50–60 cm (20–24 ins) at the shoulder and originates in Sweden, being named after a renowned hunter. It is usually worked on its own and requires good training as it can be wilful. It is a relatively uncommon breed in the British Isles.

heeler: Lancashire heeler a fairly uncommon, small, sturdy breed reaching a height of about 30 cm (12 ins) at the shoulder. The Lancashire heeler has the shape of a CORGI but has short smooth hair with the colours black and tan. This game little dog thrives on exercise and fun and makes a friendly family pet and good watchdog.

Hovawart this uncommon breed originates from the Black Forest region of Germany and was bred for farm work. It is an attractive large dog, reaching a height of 63–70 cm (25–28 ins) at the shoulder, and has a similar appearance to the more familiar setters and retrievers. The Hovawart has a fairly long coat and colours vary from black and gold to a light tan. This is an intelligent and independent dog that needs good training and plenty of exercise.

husky, Siberian husky a tough, strong and sturdy breed, standing at a height of 53–60 cm (21–24 ins) at the shoulder, with a thick coat that varies in colour but is usually shades of grey and black. In some respects it looks almost wolf-life and has two characteristic black lines running vertically down its forehead. The husky was bred to work as a member of a team, pulling a sled across the Arctic ice and snow. It is an intelligent dog, loyal to its owner, and a good watchdog, but is best suited for the work for which it was bred rather than as a household pet.

Ibizan hound an uncommon breed, originally from Catalonia and the Balearic islands of Spain, which is a tall attractive hound with a build resembling that of a greyhound. This dog stands at a height of 56–74 cm (22–29 ins) at the shoulder with a short coat coloured tan and white. One striking feature is the long, pricked-up ears, which enhance its intelligent and attractive appearance. The Ibizan hound is fleet of foot and was bred for hunting hare and rabbit. It makes a good house dog, having a friendly and good-natured temperament, but requires a great deal of exercise and is best suited to life in the countryside with an active family.

keeshond or **Dutch barge dog** a medium-sized attractive breed with an abundance of long fur of black, grey and tan. The keeshond reaches a height of about 46 cm (18 ins) at the shoulder and is thought to have been bred in Germany. The keeshond is tough and active and makes a loveable family pet but requires plenty of grooming to keep its coat in good order.

komonder an unusual and uncommon large breed with a very long, shaggy coat of thick cords of a greyish-white colour. It was originally bred in Hungary as a guard dog on farms and reaches a height of about 80 cm (32 ins) at the shoulder. It is an excellent guard dog and is very protective of its home and owners. The coat needs to be washed regularly if the dog is to live in the house, although it does not require a lot of brushing.

Leonberger an attractive although uncommon large breed originally developed in the town of Leonberg in Germany, with SAINT BERNARD, NEWFOUNDLAND and PYRENEAN MOUNTAIN DOG ancestry.

The Leonberger reaches a height of 72–80 cm (28–32 ins) at the shoulder and has a thick coat coloured gold and black. It is good-natured, intelligent and friendly, and makes a good pet for those with plenty of space and is an excellent watchdog. It thrives on an active life in the country.

lhasa apso a most attractive toy breed with abundant long, silky fur in shades of cream and grey. This little dog has an appealing face with a long 'beard' and pendulous ears. It was bred in the mountainous regions of Tibet and is game and hardy, intelligent and affectionate. The lhasa apso stands at a height of about 25 cm (10 ins). In spite of its small size, it makes a good watchdog as well as an appealing pet. Its coat requires considerable grooming and is usually parted on either side of a line running along the length of its back.

Lowchen or **Little Lion dog** a very appealing toy breed with long silky fur in shades of white, cream and black, which is usually cut in a lion clip. The Lowchen reaches a height of 25–33 cm (10–13 ins) and makes an attractive and intelligent family dog. In spite of its small size, the Lowchen is lively, fun-loving and always ready for action.

lurcher not an official breed but a 'type', the lurcher comes in a variety of coat colours and resembles a rough-haired greyhound. It is very much a dog of the countryside, traditionally associated with travelling people and also with those who made a clandestine living by poaching!

Maltese an attractive toy breed with a long coat of silky white fur and an appealing and intelligent expression. This little dog reaches a height of 25 cm (10 ins) and was originally bred on Malta. It requires a great deal of grooming to keep its coat in order, but makes a loving and lively little household pet and is always ready for activity and fun. The fur is usually parted on either side of a line running vertically along the head and back, and the Maltese usually sports a bow when in the showing ring.

mastiff a very large, powerfully built British breed with an ancient lineage that can be traced back many centuries. The mastiff reaches a height of about 76 cm (30 ins) at the shoulder and is sturdily built with a broad head and a wrinkled forehead that gives it a somewhat worried expression. It is believed to have been bred as a guard dog, and its sheer size, presence and deep bark are certainly effective. Usually, however, the mastiff is good-natured, friendly and obedient. It makes a suitable family pet for those with plenty of space, and needs lots of exercise and feeding. The colour is normally a golden brown with some black, especially around the face. Mastiffs do not usually live for longer than 10 years.

Mexican hairless or **Xoloitzcuinth** an extremely rare breed but worthy of mention for its unusual features. The dog reaches a height of about 45 cm (18 ins) at the shoulder and lacks hair except for a coarse covering on the upper part of its head. The Mexican hairless has a higher than average body temperature (in common with the Chinese crested), which is 40.5°C, compared to the 38.5°C that is the norm for all other breeds. It is unable to bark but makes an unusual crying noise. Its origins are obscure, although it is believed to have been bred in Asia.

Munsterlander: Large Munsterlander an attractive breed of gundog with a black and white coat of long fur similar to that of a BORDER COLLIE. This intelligent and hardy working dog was originally bred in Germany in the Münster region, and it reaches a height of about 61 cm (24 ins) at the shoulder. Although bred for sporting purposes in the 1920s, it is good-natured and friendly and responds well to training. It can make a good family dog but needs plenty of exercise and activity.

Newfoundland a large, sturdily built breed with an abundant, dense long coat of brownish-black fur. The Newfoundland was bred to retrieve or rescue objects or people from water. The coat is waterproofed with oil, and the skin between the toes extends as far as the claws as an adaptation for swimming. This 'webbing' between the toes is a unique feature of the 'water dogs', specifically Newfoundlands and otter hounds. The Newfoundland reaches a height of about 71 cm (28 ins) at the shoulder and is usually friendly, affectionate and playful and can make a good family pet. Care should be taken not to over-exercise a Newfoundland puppy, but in adult life the dog needs walks in order to remain fit and healthy. They are prone to rupture of the ligament of the stifle joint of the hind leg, and this can lead to later development of osteoarthritis. Because of their large size, Newfoundlands need plenty of space and feeding and are best suited to life in the country.

otter hound a large, sturdily built breed with an ancient ancestry that can be traced back to medieval times. The otter hound reaches a height of about 67 cm (27 ins) at the shoulder and has a long, shaggy coat of dense greyish coloured fur. Like the NEWFOUNDLAND, the otter hound was bred for water work, particularly retrieving, and has a well-oiled waterproof coat and 'webbed' feet. It is generally good-natured and friendly and can make a good family dog but requires plenty of space, exercise and feeding.

papillon a most attractive toy breed, which stands at a height of 20–28 cm (8–11 ins) at the shoulder. The papillon has a long coat of fine hair and is 'tortoiseshell' coloured, i.e. russet, white and black. It has pricked, triangular ears like the wings of a butterfly (*papillon* is French for 'butterfly'). It is alert, active and intelligent and makes a charming, family pet always ready for action.

Pekinese or **Pekingese** a very familiar toy breed with long silky hair in shades of cream and grey, originally bred in China. The Pekinese is like a little Chinese lion, resembling images in Far Eastern art and sculpture. It is a flat-faced, short-nosed little dog and so tends to snuffle and snort, and has a large personality for one so small. It may suffer from a condition called distichiasis, in which a double row of eyelashes causes inflammation and irritation of the eyeball. It also tends to have bulging eyeballs, which may in certain circumstances become prolapsed. The bulging eyes tend to interfere with the natural drainage of the lacrimal fluid that bathes the eyeballs, hence it tends to suffer from an overflow of 'tears', causing two wet streaks on either side of its nose. These little dogs have fast-growing claws that require regular clipping, and they are brachycephalic, i.e. puppies have a relatively large head, which can cause problems for a bitch in giving birth. Pekinese make charming, intelligent little pets but are intolerant of children. They require very little exercise or house space and are best suited to owners with plenty of time to spend on grooming.

Pharaoh hound an elegant, smooth-haired, chestnut-coloured dog with some patches of white and long, pointed pricked ears. The Pharaoh hound resembles the images depicted in ancient Egyptian art and sculpture. It is believed to be of ancient origin, but those in Britain came originally from Malta. The Pharaoh hound reaches a height of about 56 cm (22 ins) at the shoulder and is a friendly, good-natured dog, requiring little grooming but plenty of exercise and activity.

pinscher: German pinscher this breed belongs to the same group as the Doberman and is similarly coloured black and tan with the same short, smooth coat. It is of medium size, however, and reaches a height of 43–48 cm (17–19 ins) at the shoulder. The pinscher is an ancient German breed that was used as a guard dog. It is intelligent, brave and loyal to its own home and family, but needs plenty of exercise and good training. Some individuals are inclined to be forceful and dominant, but they can make good house dogs.

pinscher: miniature pinscher a toy breed, reaching a height of 25–30 cm (10–12 ins) at the shoulder, but similar in other respects to the larger pinscher. It is bold, energetic and active, and makes a good house and watchdog but needs plenty of exercise.

pointer a large, attractive breed, developed as a gundog, that reaches a height of 63–69 cm (25–27 ins) at the shoulder. It is a strong, athletic-looking dog with short hair and is usually coloured chocolate brown and white. Some may be white with brown spots or markings and a brown head. It is intelligent, friendly and affectionate, and can make an excellent family dog although it requires a great deal of exercise. It is able to 'point' at hidden game by holding its body in a straight line with the head extended and the tail held horizontally and often with one front paw raised.

pointer: German short-haired pointer the German short-haired pointer has the ability to 'point' but will also retrieve birds that have been shot. It is a large, energetic dog that reaches a height of about 58 cm (23 ins) at the shoulder. It has a smooth coat and is usually coloured chocolate brown with white markings. It is intelligent, good-natured and friendly, and makes a fine family dog although it requires plenty of space and exercise. Bitches occasionally develop eclampsia, or milk fever, after giving birth, which is unusual as this condition is rare among large breeds of dog.

pointer: German wire-haired pointer of similar colours to the short-haired breed, the wire-haired pointer is usually somewhat larger and more sturdy, reaching a height of 60–67 cm (24–26 ins) at the shoulder. It has a longer coat, which gives it good protection when it is out in all weathers, and has the same temperament and abilities as the other pointers. Once again, the main requirements for this dog are lots of space and exercise.

Pomeranian a toy breed with an abundant coat of long, fine fur coloured shades of chestnut brown and cream, the Pomeranian requires a great deal of grooming to keep its coat in order but is bright, hardy and intelligent, enjoying activity and exercise. It makes a loveable family pet and was probably originally derived from larger spitz types of dog. Pomeranian males have a tendency for the inherited condition known as cryptorchidism in which one or both testicles fail to descend. (*See also* SEXUAL BEHAVIOUR AND BREEDING—Male dog, page 44.)

poodle: French poodle instantly familiar to most people throughout the world, poodles are believed to have been originally bred in France and Germany. There are three sizes: the standard, which is over 38 cm (15 ins) at the shoulder and may be quite large; the miniature, which is less than 38 cm (15 ins) but more than 28 cm (11 ins); and the toy, which is less than 28 cm (11 ins) at the shoulder. Poodles may be either white or black in colour, and while the miniature and toy breeds have come to epitomize the typical lapdog, they were originally bred as working dogs to retrieve fallen birds from water. Poodles do not shed hair, which is an advantage in the home, especially for people who are allergic to pet hair.

The curly coat requires regular clipping, and the most popular style is the lamb clip in which the hair is cut to a uniform length all over. Another type is the Dutch clip, in which the hair on the body is cut short while that on the legs is left long so that the dog appears to be wearing baggy trousers. For the showing ring, poodles are often given the lion clip, which is said to have been devised by the French queen, Marie Antoinette. The hair on the front of the body and head is left long but the rear quarters, legs and tail are clipped close to the skin except for 'pom-poms' left at the ankles and at the end of the tail. The coat is brushed out so that it is fluffed up and stands on end. At the time of clipping, it is also necessary to remove excess hair growing inside the ear flaps along the external canal. Miniature poodles are particularly prone to blockage of the ear canal by wax, which leads to soreness and inflammation, and this problem is made worse by excess hair.

Poodles have a tendency to suffer from trichiasis, a condition in which the eyelashes grow in the wrong direction, causing irritation and inflammation of the eyes. Males have an increased risk of cryptorchidism, in which one or both testicles fail to descend. There is also increased likelihood of the development of Cushing's syndrome. Miniature poodles may suffer from an inherited congenital defect that causes the knee cap to be easily displaced, called patellar luxation. Miniature and toy poodles have an increased likelihood of epilepsy (*see* CONVULSIONS, page 91) and blockage of the lacrimal ducts, so that 'tears' run down the face, causing two brown streaks on either side of the nose (in white dogs).

In the past, some individuals, especially miniature and toy poodles, gained a reputation for being snappy, unpredictable and highly strung. On the whole, this was caused by intense over-breeding from dogs that showed these characteristics and should not have been used to satisfy the public demand for poodles. More recently, responsible breeders have endeavoured to ensure that such traits are, as far as possible, not perpetuated. Hence it can be said that poodles make charming and highly intelligent pets and enjoy exercise and activity. They should be no more or less likely to exhibit behavioural problems than any other dog and remain one of the most popular breeds.

pug or **carlin** an immensely appealing toy breed that is, nonetheless, sturdily built and full of character. The pug is one of the brachycephalic breeds, with an enormous broad head, quite small ears and a curly, pig-like tail. It has a light fawn-coloured, short coat with some black markings, especially on the face. The skin is thrown into folds and wrinkles in places, particularly on the face, and the eyes are large and protuberant. Pugs have squashed faces and short noses and suffer from the breathing problems that beset all such breeds. They tend to snuffle and snort and are susceptible to heat because of their difficulties in breathing (*see* HEATSTROKE, page 109). The large head of the puppies can cause difficulties for a pug bitch in giving birth. The folded skin, especially on the face, is liable to become hot and damp, and this may cause inflammation and infection. The round, bulging eyes are susceptible to prolapse and also tend to cause blockage of the lacrimal ducts so that 'tears' flow down the face, causing wet streaks. Pugs make loveable house pets, requiring little space or exercise, and are loyal and affectionate towards their owners.

puli: Hungarian puli an unusual, sturdy breed that was developed in Hungary for working with cattle and sheep. The puli reaches a height of 40–44 cm (16–18 ins) at the shoulder and has a long, shaggy black coat of cords that reach the ground and cover its face. In fact, one needs to look closely at this dog to see which end is which! The puli is extremely hardy and also loyal and intelligent. It can make a good house dog but needs regular bathing if it is to live in a home. It is best suited to a country home and needs plenty of exercise and activity.

Pyrenean mountain dog or **Great Pyrenees** a large, attractive breed with a long, dense coat of white fur. It reaches a height in excess of 70 cm (28 ins) at the shoulder and was bred for guarding sheep flocks from attacks by wolves. It is bold, courageous and hardy, with a coat able to withstand the most extreme weather conditions. Also, it is gentle and affectionate and makes a good family pet, guard and watchdog. It is intelligent and responsive to training, and is unusual in that it possesses double dew claws on its hind limbs (in common with the BRIARD). It needs plenty of exercise, space and grooming to keep its coat in good order.

retriever: Chesapeake Bay retriever a large, sturdy retriever, originally bred in Maryland in the USA. It is thought that the ancestors of the breed include NEWFOUNDLANDS or LABRADOR retrievers , which were introduced to this area following a shipwreck in the early 1800s. These were then crossed with native breeds to produce the Chesapeake Bay retriever. These dogs reach a height of 59–66 cm (23–26 ins) at the shoulder and have a short dense coat of golden brown fur. They are good-natured and affectionate family dogs, but have an independent streak and so require firm training. They are best suited to an outdoor country life, requiring plenty of exercise and making good watchdogs.

retriever: curly-coated retriever a sturdy, large breed of gundog that stands at a height of about 69 cm (28 ins) at the shoulder. This dog has a waterproof curly coat coloured dark brown or black and was bred for retrieving fallen birds from water. It can make a friendly and affectionate house dog but requires plenty of exercise and grooming to keep its coat in good order. It is also a good watch and guard dog. It is probably best suited to an active country life with experienced owners.

retriever: flat-coated retriever this breed resembles the golden retriever in size and build but has a black coat of fairly long, dense hair. It was bred as a gundog and is intelligent and willing to work, enjoying exercise and activity. It reaches a height of about 58–61 cm (23–24 ins) at the shoulder and is good-natured and affectionate, making an excellent family dog and watchdog. It needs plenty of space and exercise and is probably happiest in a country home.

retriever: golden retriever one of the most familiar and best-loved breeds, which excels in many spheres. They have long coats of yellow-brown and cream and require regular grooming. The average height at the shoulder is in the order of 56–61 cm (22–24 ins). Golden retrievers make excellent family pets, being good-natured, eager to please, affectionate and tolerant. They enjoy walks, activities and being with their family. They are calm and intelligent and keen to learn, and have become popular as guide dogs for the blind and 'hearing dogs' for the deaf. Also, they are used in police work and in mountain rescue, and thoroughly deserve their popular reputation. They are susceptible to the eye disorder known as progressive retinal atrophy, which tends to affect the centre of the eyes first and leads to a worsening of vision.

retriever: Labrador retriever another familiar and highly popular breed with an excellent temperament. The Labrador is sturdily built and reaches a height of 56–57 cm (22 ins) at the shoulder. It was bred to retrieve fallen birds at a shoot and excels at this work, being happy to enter water. It may be either golden or black in colour with a short, dense coat. Labradors have an easy-going, affectionate and willing disposition and are intelligent and easy to train. They are used in all the same spheres as the golden retriever, i.e. as guide and hearing dogs and in police, army and forensic work.

Labradors make ideal family dogs but need plenty of exercise and careful feeding as they are inclined to obesity, especially in old age. They enjoy life in the country and being part of the family.

Rhodesian ridgeback an attractive and unusual large breed that stands at a height of about 67 cm (27 ins) at the shoulder. It has a short coat of golden brown hair and a ridge along the centre of the back formed from hair growing in the opposite direction. This forms two distinct whorls on the shoulders of the dog. It is an intelligent, alert and active dog, needing plenty of exercise and good training. It can make a good family dog but needs plenty of space. Uniquely, Rhodesian ridgebacks may develop one or more dermoid sinuses, which are tube-like structures, often infected and with thick walls, that break open onto the surface of the skin. These powerful animals have well-developed guarding instincts and are highly effective as watchdogs.

Rottweiler an impressive, large and muscular dog that reaches a height of 63–69 cm (25–27 ins) at the shoulder. It has a short dense coat and is mainly black but with some tan on the face and legs. It is powerfully built with a broad head. In recent years, they have become notorious because some individual dogs have severely attacked and even killed children. Some experts believe that this has arisen through irresponsible breeding from dogs showing aggressive tendencies. In some cases aggressive traits have been encouraged in Rottweilers, especially in those used as guard dogs. In fact, most of these dogs are calm, good-natured, affectionate and wishing to please and are intelligent and easy to train. They can make good house dogs but need plenty of space and exercise and, above all, responsible owners. Anyone considering acquiring a Rottweiler should be thoroughly satisfied with the credentials and good reputation of the breeder before taking on a puppy.

Saint Bernard an enormous, tall dog, reaching at least 76 cm (30 ins) at the shoulder, that is another familiar and much loved breed with an interesting history. They have a thick coat of fairly long fur coloured chestnut brown and white. They have an acute, well-developed sense of smell and were used to locate people buried by avalanches in the Swiss Alps. They were kept by the monks of the hospice at the head of the Great Saint Bernard Pass and used

to locate people lost in snowstorms. They have a gentle, affectionate nature and can make good family dogs, although they require
plenty of room, feeding and exercise. They are best suited to life in
the country or where there is plenty of open space. The average life
span, in common with most of the other large breeds, is around ten
years, and care must be taken not to over-exercise a Saint Bernard
puppy as this can cause permanent joint damage. Saint Bernards
are prone to a disorder of the eyelids called entropion (*see* page
103). The lids curl outwards, exposing the surface of the eyeball
and causing irritation and excessive watering.

Saluki or **Persian greyhound** resembling a long-haired greyhound but with more pendulous ears, the Saluki is a fast, lean aristocratic-looking hound bred for the chase. The breed was developed in the Middle East for hunting quarry such as gazelles and
jackals, and is usually coloured tan and white with shades of grey.
It reaches a height of 59–71 cm (23–28 ins) at the shoulder and has
a long, feathery tail and ears. The Saluki is very active and intelligent and requires a great deal of exercise but can be independent in
nature. It is best suited to owners with plenty of time and energy to
keep it fully occupied.

Samoyed a very attractive medium-sized breed with an abundant
coat of thick, long white fur. The dog was bred for work in the cold
steppes of Russia as a farm, hunting and guard dog. The Samoyed
reaches a height of 51–56 cm (20–22 ins) at the shoulder and carries its tail curled over its back. It is intelligent, active and good-
natured but requires a great deal of grooming to keep its coat in
good order.

schipperke a small, hardy, spitz breed with pointed, pricked ears
and fox-like face and a thick coat of black fur. It was bred in Flan-
ders as a ratter and is lively, courageous and intelligent. It makes an
affectionate family dog, always ready for exercise and activity.

schnauzer a medium-sized, square-faced German breed that is
strong, brave and intelligent. It reaches a height of 48 cm (19 ins) at
the shoulder and has a tough, wiry coat in shades of grey and
cream. It is friendly and affectionate towards its own family but
tends to be wary of strangers. It needs plenty of exercise and activity, and its coat requires regular grooming, stripping and trimming.

schnauzer: miniature schnauzer a smaller version of the schnauzer with a similar build and type of coat but reaching a height of 36 cm (14 ins) at the shoulder. It is intelligent, hardy, loving and active and responds well to training. It makes a good family dog and watchdog and is always ready for walks and activity. Miniature schnauzers are sometimes affected by hereditary cataracts of the eyes, which can result in blindness.

schnauzer: giant schnauzer an impressive, tall schnauzer that reaches a height of 65–70 cm (26–28 ins) at the shoulder. It is a tough, hardy dog, bred in Bavaria for cattle droving and as a farm guard, and is brave and intelligent. The wiry coat is often black in colour, although it may also be shades of grey. The giant schnauzer needs firm training and plenty of exercise and can make a good house dog and watchdog.

setter: English setter an attractive, tall, lean breed developed as a gundog but with a loveable, playful friendly personality that makes it an endearing family pet. The English setter stands at a height of 65–68 cm (26–27 ins) at the shoulder and has a long coat, coloured white or cream with streaks of grey. It has 'feathers' on the legs and tail, and needs some time spent on grooming to keep the coat in good order. The English setter loves walks and activity and is best suited to a country home with plenty of space.

setter: Gordon setter a very attractive breed of gundog with a long coat coloured black and tan. It reaches a height of about 66 cm (26 ins) at the shoulder and is somewhat more solidly built than either the ENGLISH or IRISH SETTER. It is good-natured, friendly and affectionate and can make a loveable family pet. Like all the setters, it needs plenty of exercise and activity and time spent on grooming, and is best suited to the country life.

setter: Irish setter or **red setter** a familiar and much loved breed, instantly recognizable because of its attractive, long and glossy, chestnut brown coat. The Irish setter was bred as a gundog built for speed and agility, and it reaches a height of about 66 cm (26 ins) at the shoulder. It has abundant energy and needs a great deal of exercise. It is playful, affectionate and good-natured, always ready for walks and activity. Its coat needs regular grooming to keep it in good order, and the Irish setter needs a country home with plenty of space in which to romp and play. Irish setters are prone to a progressive degeneration of the retina of the eye, which leads to a deterioration in vision.

setter: Irish red and white setter a much less common breed of setter, coloured white and red and reaching a height of about 66 cm (26 ins) at the shoulder. It shares the same happy, good-natured and affectionate disposition as the other setters and makes a good family pet. It is ideally suited to life in the country with plenty of walks and exercise.

Shar Pei or **Chinese fighting dog** one of the most unusual and, until recently, rare and exotic breeds, which has been saved from extinction by renewed interest and increased breeding. It is a medium-sized, sturdily built dog with a broad head and square face and reaches a height of 46–51 cm (18–20 ins) at the shoulder. Its most notable feature is that it has a skin that is thrown into numerous folds and wrinkles and is covered by short, bristly stubble, coloured light grey and fawn. A Shar Pei tends to have a mind of its own but can make a loyal, brave and loveable house dog and a pet that will excite interest and comment.

sheepdog: Maremma sheepdog an uncommon breed of large dog, originally from Italy, that reaches a height of 65–73 cm (26–29 ins) at the shoulder. It has a thick and fairly long coat in a creamy fawn colour and is fearless and powerful. It was bred to herd and guard flocks and is highly intelligent although rather independent in nature. It is best suited to experienced owners and needs plenty of exercise and to be kept fully occupied.

sheepdog: Old English sheepdog another familiar and much loved ancient breed that has been made famous through its association with one particular widely advertised brand of paint. This association has been so effective that it is worth remembering that the Old English sheepdog was, in fact, bred for guarding and herding flocks. It reaches a height of about 61 cm (24 ins) at the shoulder and has a long, thick coat of fur, coloured white and grey, that covers its face. The abundant coat needs a great deal of time and attention on grooming, and since it is so thick, the dog is very susceptible to heat (*see* HEATSTROKE, page 109). In the summer months, the Old English is more comfortable if its coat is clipped, and this can certainly be done if the dog is not being exhibited at shows. The Old English sheepdog is intelligent, affectionate and lively and makes a good family pet. It does, however, require plenty of exercise, activity and space, and is ideally suited to life in the country. Old English sheepdogs can be affected by hereditary cataracts, which are a cause of blindness. Some individuals may be inclined to suffer from recurrent bouts of diarrhoea and need careful feeding.

sheepdog: Polish lowland sheepdog an unusual breed of sturdy sheepdog originating in Poland and used for shepherding and farm work. The Polish lowland sheepdog is of medium size, reaching a height of about 43–52 cm (17–20 ins) at the shoulder, and has a thick coat of long fur coloured white and grey. It is an intelligent, friendly and active dog, ideal for a family, but needs a considerable amount of grooming to keep its coat in good order.

sheepdog: Shetland sheepdog a smaller version of the rough collie, standing at a height of about 37 cm (14–15 ins) at the shoulder. The Shetland sheepdog has a beautiful long coat in shades of tan, white and black, and needs a great deal of grooming to keep it looking its best. It is a bright, good-natured and charming dog that makes an ideal family pet, although it may try to 'round up' pets or children! It enjoys walks and being part of a family. It is susceptible to a degenerative condition of the retina of the eyes leading to a loss of vision.

shepherd dog: Anatolian shepherd dog an unusual breed of very large and powerful sheepdog used for herding and guarding flocks and farms in its native Turkey. It reaches a height of about 81 cm (31 ins) at the shoulder and has a coat of cream-coloured thick fur with white on the chest and underside and a dark muzzle and ears. It is an intelligent, active and independent dog, requiring firm training. It is best suited to experienced owners with plenty of time to devote to its training and exercise.

shepherd dog: Belgian shepherd dog this breed resembles the German shepherd but is far less common in Britain. It reaches a height of 61–66 cm (24–26 ins) at the shoulder, and there are four varieties, two of which have a coat of long, thick fur. The Groennendael is coloured black, and the Terveuren is golden brown with a dark muzzle and ears. The Laekenois has a wiry coat while the

Malinois is a short-haired variety. All are intelligent, responsive and active dogs that require firm training and plenty of exercise and work to keep them fully occupied. They are best suited to experienced owners with plenty of time to devote to their dog.

shepherd dog: German shepherd dog or **Alsatian** a very familiar breed, and the most popular on a worldwide basis, that was originally developed in Germany for herding and guarding. The German shepherd has a thick coat coloured tan and black, upright ears and an alert and intelligent expression. Its intelligence has been utilized by police and army forces throughout the world, and it has been trained to carry out a number of difficult tasks. It is also popular as a house dog and is loyal and affectionate towards its owners. Some individuals have given the breed a reputation for aggression. Once again, much of this is probably attributable to irresponsible breeding and inappropriate treatment. If from a good background and well treated and handled, the German shepherd should be no more inclined to be aggressive than any other breed. In common with other large breeds, some individuals are inclined to hip dysplasia, and persistent diarrhoea is another recognized problem. The masticatory muscles that operate the jaws may become tender and inflamed so that it is painful for the dog to eat. German shepherds are inclined to produce an excessive amount of ear wax, which can be responsible for inflammation and soreness. There may be an excessive secretion of fluid from the nasal gland, which drips from the nose when the dog is stressed or excited. German shepherds reach a height of 63 cm (25 ins) at the shoulder and are active and powerful, needing good training and plenty of exercise. Bitches of the breed seem to have the shortest intervals between periods of heat, on average about 26 weeks.

shih-tzu a very attractive little Chinese breed that stands at a height of about 27 cm (11 ins) at the shoulder. The shih-tzu has a long silky coat in shades of grey, which reaches the ground, with tan coloured 'whiskers' and 'beard'. It is alert, bright, active and affectionate, and makes a good family pet and watchdog in spite of its small size. The coat needs a great deal of grooming to keep it in good order, but the shih-tzu does not require much in the way of space and exercise.

Shibu Inu: Japanese Shibu Inu a sturdy, medium-sized Japanese breed looking a little like a short-haired, lean chow-chow. The Shibu Inu reaches a height of about 40 cm (16 ins) at the shoulder and has a dense coat of chestnut gold and white, pricked ears and a tail tightly curled over its back. This attractive dog is alert, intelligent and friendly and makes an unusual pet and a good watchdog.

spaniel: clumber spaniel a heavily built spaniel with a long, thick coat of silky, white fur. It was bred for both flushing out game birds and retrieving them and came originally from France. It is named, however, after Clumber Park in Nottinghamshire, the ancestral home of the dukes of Newcastle, some dogs of the breed having been brought there after the French Revolution. It has a quiet, determined and somewhat aloof nature but can make a good and faithful house dog. The coat requires regular grooming and bathing to keep it looking tidy, with occasional stripping out of dead hair.

spaniel: cocker spaniel the cocker spaniel is another highly popular and much loved breed, which was originally developed as a working gundog. It was particularly bred for the putting up of woodcock ('cocking') from which the name is derived. The cocker spaniel has a long, silky, wavy coat coloured either golden brown or black and reaches a height of 39–41 cm (15–16 ins) at the shoulder. All spaniels tend to have a greasy coat because of excess secretion of an oily substance called sebum from the sebaceous glands in the skin, which has a protective and waterproofing function. Hence the cocker spaniel should be bathed frequently and the coat groomed regularly or the dog is liable to become smelly. Particular attention needs to be given to the long, drooping ears of this spaniel as they are prone to various ear disorders. The coat also benefits from occasional clipping and stripping away of dead hairs. Cocker spaniels are good-natured, friendly and affectionate and make excellent family dogs. They need plenty of exercise and activity and careful feeding as they are inclined to become obese. Occasionally some individuals may develop an inherited form of glaucoma caused by a build-up of fluid within the eye. All spaniels are somewhat more prone to develop epilepsy (*see* CONVULSIONS, page 91) than most other breeds of dog.

spaniel: American cocker spaniel a slightly smaller breed than the cocker spaniel with a higher, domed head and a more dense coat. The American cocker spaniel reaches a height of 36–39 cm (14–15 ins) at the shoulder and has abundant, long, silky, wavy fur that requires a great deal of grooming. It also needs regular trimming and stripping away of dead hair and frequent bathing. The American cocker shares the same cheerful and friendly disposition as the other spaniels and makes an affectionate family pet, one that is always ready to join in with walks and other activities. Some individuals can develop hereditary cataracts.

spaniel: field spaniel a sturdy, robust breed of gundog that reaches a height of about 46 cm (18 ins) at the shoulder and has a long, curly coat coloured chocolate brown. It has an affectionate and friendly nature and enjoys work, exercise and activity. It is best suited to life in the country, and its coat requires regular grooming and bathing to keep it in good order.

spaniel: King Charles spaniel a very attractive toy breed that was popular in the royal household of King Charles II and features in paintings from that period. The King Charles is coloured black, white and brown, and has a long, silky, wavy coat that requires regular grooming and bathing. It has a most attractive, short, squashed face and large, soulful eyes, and is intelligent, lively, affectionate and friendly. It makes an ideal pet and requires less in the way of space and exercise than the larger spaniels.

spaniel: Cavalier King Charles spaniel a slightly larger version of the KING CHARLES SPANIEL and derived from it by selective breeding. This little dog has a flatter head and longer nose than its ancestor but its coat type and coloration are similar. It is happy, affectionate and good-natured, enjoying all activities, and makes an excellent family pet.

spaniel: English springer spaniel another much loved breed popular both as a working gundog and as a family pet. The English springer spaniel reaches a height of about 51 cm (20 ins) at the shoulder, and has a long, silky, wavy coat coloured chocolate brown and white or black and white. It is a very active dog and will run about all day long and still be ready for more. The English springer is happy, affectionate and friendly and easy to train, and makes an ideal family pet. It is an excellent dog for those who enjoy long walks in the countryside and, like all spaniels, requires regular grooming and bathing.

spaniel: Welsh springer spaniel a slightly smaller and more finely made breed than the English springer, reaching a height of about 48 cm (19 ins) at the shoulder. Its nature, coat colours and type are similar to the English springer, and it makes an ideal family pet in an active household as well as an indefatigable working gundog.

spaniel: Sussex spaniel a solidly built breed with a short face and somewhat more worried expression than some of the other more happy-go-lucky spaniels. It has a chocolate coloured, glossy, long coat that requires regular grooming and bathing. It has a friendly and obedient disposition and can make a good family pet as well as a useful gundog.

spaniel: Tibetan spaniel a toy breed that does not resemble the other spaniels but is a lively, bright and active little dog with a mind of its own. It has a creamy coloured, light tan coat of long fur and a dark muzzle, and it makes a most appealing pet.

spaniel: Irish water spaniel a tall, unusual looking spaniel with a long, shaggy, curly coat resembling that of a poodle. The Irish water spaniel reaches a height of 53–58 cm (21–23 ins) at the shoulder and is coloured dark brown. As the name suggests, it loves the water and was bred to retrieve fallen game birds from lakes and marshes. It is hardy, friendly and affectionate, and makes a good family pet as well as a useful gundog.

Spinone: Italian Spinone an unusual breed of large gundog that was bred in the north of Italy although its ancestors were taken there from France. The Spinone reaches a height of 60–70 cm (24–28 ins) at the shoulder, and it is a strong animal with a wiry coat, usually coloured creamy fawn. It is a good-natured and placid breed, which can make an unusual family pet as well as a working dog.

spitz: Finnish spitz an attractive medium-sized breed showing typical characteristics of the spitz type of dog. The Finnish spitz has pricked, pointed ears and a fox-like face and a thick, long coat coloured reddish gold. The tail is carried tightly curled over the end of its back, and it is bold, intelligent and hardy with a mind of its own. The Finnish spitz makes a good house and watchdog and enjoys exercise and activity.

spitz: German spitz the German spitz is an attractive breed that varies in size from small to medium, i.e. from about 23 cm (9 ins) to 36 cm (14 ins) at the shoulder. It has a long, thick coat coloured shades of grey, black and cream, and carries its feathery tail curled tightly over its back. It has the somewhat fox-like face and pricked, pointed ears of the spitz breeds and shares their bold, intelligent, active nature. The German spitz makes a most attractive, hardy pet, enjoying walks and activities as well as being a good little watchdog.

spitz: Japanese spitz resembling a smaller version of the Russian SAMOYED, the Japanese spitz has a beautiful coat of long, white fur and reaches a height of 30–36 cm (12–14 ins) at the shoulder. It has the foxy face and pricked, pointed ears that are characteristic of the spitz breeds and the same intelligent, active and independent nature. This little dog makes a good family pet and watchdog although its coat needs considerable grooming to keep it looking its best.

terrier: Airedale terrier a distinctive breed and the biggest type of terrier, the Airedale reaches a height of 58–61 cm (23–24 ins) at the shoulder. It has a wiry, curly coat coloured black and tan, which requires occasional clipping and stripping out of dead hair. The Airedale has a square face and the breed originated in Yorkshire, where they were used for otter hunting. This hardy, bold terrier is alert and intelligent and makes a loving family pet and a good watchdog.

terrier: Australian terrier the Australian terrier is a small breed that resembles the Yorkshire terrier in the nature and colour of its coat. It is a bright, bold and intelligent little dog, reaching a height of 25 cm (10 ins) at the shoulder. It makes an affectionate family pet and one that is always ready for action and is also a good little watchdog.

terrier: Australian silky terrier this tough little toy dog was derived from crossing Yorkshire terriers with Australian terriers. It is a bright, alert and game little dog that makes an excellent family pet, one that is always ready for walks and activities. Its coat colours reveal its origins, being a combination of dark grey and tan.

terrier: Bedlington terrier an unusual looking breed that comes from Northumberland where it was developed for the hunting of rabbits and rats. It is medium-sized, reaching a height of about 41 cm (16 ins) at the shoulder, and has the shape of a whippet but with a broader face and Roman nose. Its coat resembles that of a white poodle and is not shed so needs to be clipped regularly. The Bedlington is an active, intelligent and affectionate dog that makes a good family pet, one that is always ready for walks and activities. Bedlingtons occasionally suffer from a unique form of hepatitis caused by an excess storage of copper in the liver. During development, the openings of the lacrimal ducts may rarely fail to develop so that tears formed to lubricate the eyeballs cannot drain away. The fluid overflows down the dog's face, and the condition requires corrective surgery.

terrier: Boston terrier a well-built, tough little terrier with a broad head and squashed, shortened nose, which would seem to indicate some relationship with the bulldog. It has a short coat of a dark, brindled colour and white, and pointed, pricked ears. It is intelligent, active and affectionate and can make a loveable family pet that is always game for fun and activity. Boston terriers are somewhat prone to the development of hereditary cataracts and tumours, some of which can be malignant.

terrier: bull terrier a strong and sturdily built terrier that varies in height and weight and is descended from fighting breeds. It has a very short coat, often coloured mainly white but may have some patches of brown or black. It has erect, pointed ears and a Roman nose and is a popular and familiar breed. Bull terriers are normally affectionate and obedient with people and good with children but are inclined to fight with other dogs. They can make good and loveable family pets but require firm, responsible ownership. Bull terriers, especially those that are white, are prone to a form of deafness linked to coat colour.

terrier: miniature bull terrier identical in nature and characteristics to the larger form but of a smaller size, i.e. not exceeding 35.5 cm (14 ins) at the shoulder.

terrier: Staffordshire bull terrier a well-built, sturdy, medium-sized breed standing at a height of 36–41 cm (14–16 ins) at the shoulder. 'Staffs' have a short coat, often tan coloured, a broad head and fairly short face, and were derived from fighting breeds. They are affectionate, intelligent and obedient with people and good with children, and so can make loveable family pets. They are inclined to fight with other dogs, however, and are formidable, powerful opponents. Obviously, these tendencies must be taken into account, and care is needed when exercising a Staffordshire to make sure that it is not likely to get into a fight

terrier: cairn terrier a tough little breed of wire-coated terrier coloured tan and with a dark muzzle and ears. The cairn reaches a height of 28–31 cm (11–12 ins) at the shoulder and was bred in the Scottish Highlands for fox, badger and otter hunting. It is active, brave and intelligent and makes an affectionate family dog always ready for walks and activities.

terrier: Dandie Dinmont terrier another small Scottish breed of tough and active terrier with a rough coat coloured shades of grey and gold. Its unusual name is derived from the Waverley novel *Guy Mannering* by Sir Walter Scott as the character Dandie Dinmont in the story kept these little terriers. They are intelligent, game and affectionate and make excellent family pets.

terrier: smooth fox terrier a small breed of terrier bred, as the name suggests, to accompany the hunt and go down after foxes that went to earth. The fox terrier is brave, agile, quick and determined, with a smooth coat coloured white with patches of tan or black. It has a long, narrow face and is intelligent and affectionate, making a good family pet and one that enjoys walks and activities. All fox terriers are somewhat prone to a painful eye disorder called lens luxation. The lens suddenly slips out of place, causing pain and visual disturbance. Fox terrier bitches may develop mammary tumours that can sometimes be malignant. Some individuals may be affected by an inherited form of deafness.

terrier: wire fox terrier similar in all respects to the smooth breed but with a thick, wiry coat. The wire fox terrier makes a lively, affectionate and brave family pet. Fox terriers like to hunt and are excellent ratters.

terrier: Glen of Imaal terrier an unusual Irish breed of small terrier, reaching a height of 35–36 cm (14 ins) at the shoulder. It is a hardy, active little dog with a long, shaggy coat in shades of greyish fawn. Its name comes from the glen in County Wicklow where the breed was first developed. These little terriers are affectionate and obedient and make excellent and lively family pets.

terrier: Irish terrier a tall, distinctive looking terrier that reaches a height of about 48 cm (19 ins) at the shoulder. The Irish terrier has a rough, wiry coat of an unusual red-brick colour and is intelligent and active. It is loving and obedient with people, and so makes a good family pet and watchdog. Some individuals may be inclined to fight with other dogs, so good training and firm handling are needed. Irish terriers are prone to the formation of a particular type of bladder stones.

terrier: Jack Russell terrier this familiar and popular breed of small terrier was recognized officially only in 1990, prior to that being regarded as a 'type'. The Jack Russell is a small terrier, reaching a height of about 35 cm (14 ins) at the shoulder. It has a short, smooth coat coloured mainly white but with patches of tan or black. It was first bred by a parson of the same name during the 19th century. Jack Russells like to hunt and are intelligent, active and independent. They are affectionate towards their own family but can be snappy with strangers and make excellent little guard dogs. Jack Russells require careful feeding as they are inclined to become obese, especially if not given sufficient exercise. They are somewhat prone to a painful eye disorder called lens luxation in which the lens suddenly slips out of place, causing visual disturbance.

terrier: Kerry blue terrier an attractive and unusual breed of large terrier that stands at a height of 46–48 cm (18–19 ins) at the shoulder. The Kerry blue has long, thick, curly, silky fur that is not shed and is attractively coloured a bluish slate-grey. This dog was bred as a hunter of fox, otter and badger, and is intelligent, hardy and brave. It is an affectionate and obedient family pet and an excellent watchdog. The coat requires occasional stripping and clipping to keep it in good order.

terrier: Lakeland terrier in some respects, this breed resembles a small AIREDALE but it does not exceed a height of 37 cm (14 ins) at the shoulder. It was originally bred in the Lake District as a hunter of rats and foxes and has a longish coat coloured black and tan. It is hardy, intelligent, affectionate and playful, and makes a lively pet and good watchdog.

terrier: Manchester terrier a finely built, medium-sized breed of terrier that reaches a height of 40–41 cm (16 ins) at the shoulder. It has a smooth, glossy coat of black and tan, and was bred as a ratter. It is lively, intelligent and active with a somewhat independent nature. Manchester terriers make friendly, alert and game house dogs, always ready for walks and activities.

terrier: Norfolk and Norwich terrier two breeds that are identical in all respects except that the Norwich has pricked, and the Norfolk dropped ears. These are typical small working terriers that were bred to hunt rats, foxes and badgers. They reach a height of 25–26 cm (10 ins) and have a rough coat, coloured tan. They are intelligent, active, faithful house dogs and watchdogs that like to have plenty to do.

terrier: Scottish terrier a small, sturdily built breed that originally came from the northeast of Scotland. The familiar 'Scottie' has a long, wiry coat of black fur and has been reproduced in many forms as a souvenir of Scotland, often sporting a tartan bow. This tough, determined terrier was bred as a hunter of rats and foxes, and is intelligent, alert and brave. The Scottie tends to be intolerant of children but can make a faithful friend and watchdog. The coat requires occasional clipping and strimming out of dead hair to keep it looking its best. The breed has one or two unique feature. For instance, after hard exercise the muscles may go into painful spasm, known as 'Scottie cramp'. Males have a very large prostate gland in relation to their size, and bitches tend to have difficulty in giving birth to their puppies. Some individuals may suffer from an inherited form of deafness.

terrier: Sealyham terrier a small Welsh terrier that is named after Sealyham House, Haverfordwest, where the breed was developed. The Sealyham reaches a height of 31 cm (12 ins) at the shoulder and has a long, silky coat of white fur. It is charming, friendly and intelligent but at the same time, bold and independent like the other terrier breeds. It makes an excellent friend and watchdog, but some individuals may suffer from an inherited form of deafness that is related to the white coloration. Sealyhams may occasionally suffer from a painful eye disorder called lens luxation. The lens suddenly slips out of place, causing pain and visual disturbance. Bitches of this breed may experience difficulties in delivering puppies.

terrier: Skye terrier a small terrier, originally from the island of Skye, that stands at a height of 25–26 cm (10 ins) at the shoulder. The Skye terrier has a long, silky coat that reaches the ground and covers the face and is coloured dark grey. It has quite a long body in relation to its height and is intelligent, determined and hardy. The Skye terrier tends to become attached to one owner and so is less suited to be a family pet. It tends to be unsure of strangers and makes an excellent little guard dog. The coat requires considerable grooming to keep it in good order.

terrier: Tibetan terrier this medium-sized breed is not a terrier at all but was bred to drive cattle in the high mountains of Tibet. It stands at a height of 37–41 cm (14–16 ins) at the shoulder and has a thick, long coat reaching almost to the ground and covering its face. The coat requires considerable grooming and bathing, and colours may be all white or black and white. It becomes attached to one owner and is unsure of strangers. It is an intelligent and hardy dog that enjoys the company of its owner.

terrier: English toy terrier a finely built toy terrier that reaches a height of 25–30 cm (10–12 ins) at the shoulder. The toy terrier looks like a small MANCHESTER TERRIER and was derived from this breed. It has a smooth, short coat, coloured black and tan, and pricked, pointed ears. It is alert, intelligent and active and affectionate towards its own family while rather unsure of strangers. It is a lively little dog, enjoying walks and activity, and an able watchdog in spite of its small size.

terrier: Welsh terrier this Welsh breed is similar to the LAKELAND TERRIER in appearance, although somewhat larger, reaching a height of 39 cm (16 ins) at the shoulder. It has a wiry coat, coloured black and tan, and was bred as a ratter, fox and otter hunter. It is intelligent, hardy, brave and active with an affectionate nature. It makes a faithful and obedient family pet and one always ready for action.

terrier: West Highland white terrier a most endearing and popular Scottish breed of small terrier, which does not require much in the way of space and exercise. The 'Westie' is intelligent, affectionate and lively, and makes an excellent family pet. It needs a considerable amount of grooming and regular stripping out of dead hairs to keep its coat in good order but is a charming and loveable companion.

terrier: soft-coated wheaten terrier an unusual, large sturdy Irish breed with a long, wavy coat, coloured light gold, that covers its face. It was bred to work with cattle as well as for hunting around the farm, and is hardy, good-natured and intelligent. It makes a fine family pet and good watchdog and, while needing some grooming, the coat is fairly easy to maintain in good order.

terrier: Yorkshire terrier a very familiar and popular toy breed, the 'Yorkie' is bright, alert, friendly and fun-loving, and makes an excellent family pet. It has a long, silky coat, coloured dark grey and tan, that needs a considerable amount of grooming. The coat is usually parted on either side of a line along the middle of the head and back, with a bow tied at the forehead. In spite of its toy status, the Yorkie is game for anything but does not need much in the way of space and exercise. Males may have the condition known as cryptorchidism in which one or both testicles fail to descend (*see* SEXUAL BEHAVIOUR AND BREEDING—Male dog, page 44).

Vallhund: Swedish Vallhund a sturdy, medium-sized breed with some resemblance to the corgi, bred for farm work in its native Sweden. The Vallhund is stockily built and resilient, reaching a height of 33–35 cm (13–14 ins) at the shoulder. It has a thick coat, coloured shades of grey, cream and fawn, and is friendly and intelligent. It can make a good house and watchdog and a faithful companion.

vizsla: Hungarian vizsla a large, attractive and unusual breed of gundog that is used both to point and retrieve. The vizsla reaches a height of 57–64 cm (23–25 ins) at the shoulder and has a short, sleek coat coloured reddish tan. It is good-natured, obedient and eager to please, and makes an excellent family pet as well as a working dog, but needs plenty of space and exercise.

water dog: Portuguese water dog a most unusual Portuguese breed, originally used for hunting and with a thick, woolly water-proof coat that is not shed. It reaches a height of 50–57 cm (20–23 ins) at the shoulder and is hardy and intelligent. It needs good training as it can be wilful but can make a faithful house dog and watchdog.

Weimaraner a large German breed of gundog with unusual, light-coloured eyes. The Weimaraner reaches a height of 61–69 cm (24–27 ins) at the shoulder and has a short, sleek coat of light grey-fawn. It is usually good-natured and well behaved, although it can be unsure of strangers. It can make a good house dog but needs plenty of space and exercise. It is also an excellent watchdog.

whippet like a small greyhound and with similar speed and athleticism, the whippet was originally bred for rabbit hunting. It reaches a height of 47–51 cm (18–20 ins) at the shoulder and has a short sleek coat of variable colours including grey, fawn and white. The whippet is a charming, intelligent dog, which is very good-natured and makes an excellent family pet. It enjoys activity and needs plenty of walks and exercise. Its lean build and short, fine coat make it susceptible to cold, and it needs protection in harsh weather conditions.

wolfhound: Irish wolfhound a majestic ancient breed of large hound that was originally used in much the same way as the Scottish DEERHOUND for hunting wolves, bears and other large quarry. The two breeds are very similar in appearance and probably share some common ancestry. The wolfhound reaches a height of at least 79 cm (31 ins) at the shoulder and has a long, shaggy coat of a greyish fawn colour. It is intelligent, obedient and friendly but obviously requires plenty of space and a great deal of feeding. It is best suited to a large home in the country.